Praise for Jay Hammond's
TALE'S OF ALASKA'S
BUSH RAT GOVERNOR

"Jay Hammond is a unique figure in U.S.
politics...A good read by a good man."
—President George Bush

" ...entertaining, informative and challenging:
a rare combination for an autobiography...
Hammond's experiences in Alaska are
described with inimitable style."
—President Jimmy Carter

"I wish every American could read it. It would
go a long way to restoring confidence in their fellow man, if not
in politicians."
—Chuck Colson

"A joy to read. Once you pick up this book it
will be hard to put down."
—*Sitka* (Alaska) *Daily Sentinel*

"...without guestion the most entertaining
autobiography I've read. So impressed I
bought 7 additional copies..."
—Paul A. Berrett, Atty

"I don't know when I've laughed as
hard or as much."
—*News Tribune*, Tacoma, WA

CHIPS *from the* CHOPPING BLOCK
JAY HAMMOND
More Tales from Alaska's
Bush Rat Governor

Foreword by JIM REARDEN

Warm wishes from Alaska to Lin.

Jay Hammond

2/1/02

EPICENTER PRESS
Alaska Book Adventures

Epicenter Press is a regional press founded in Alaska whose interests include but are not limited to the arts, history, nature, and diverse cultures and lifestyles of the North Pacific and high latitudes. Epicenter seeks both the traditional and innovative in publishing high-quality nonfiction books and contemporary art and photography gift books.

Publisher: Kent Sturgis
Editor: Don Graydon
Cover Design: Elizabeth Watson, Watson Design
Text design: Victoria Sturgis
Proofreader: Sherrill Carlson
Printer: CDS Documentation

Library of Congress Control Number: 2001097661
ISBN 0-9708493-5-4

To order extra copies of CHIPS FROM THE CHOPPING BLOCK, mail $14.95 plus $4.95 to Epicenter Press, Box 82368, Kenmore, WA 98028. WA residents add $1.50 for state sales tax. You also may order via fax to (425) 481-8253, via phone to (800) 950-6663, or at our website, EpicenterPress.com.

Booksellers: Retail discounts are available from our trade distributor, Graphic Arts Center Publishing™, Box 10306, Portland, OR 97210.

First Edition
First printing November 2001

10 9 8 7 6 5 4 3 2 1

This book is dedicated to three fine Alaskans—Bob Atwood, Wally Hickel, and Red Boucher—who inspired some of its content by verbally clawing at my flanks in the old days. Though political opponents when I targeted them in my earlier autobiography, they all seemingly later forgave me—or perhaps they simply forgot. In reminding them again of past insults, I hope the cherished friendships evolving since then will not dissolve in the acrimony in which those affronts were originally steeped. With gratitude for their having made my life so much more zestful and broadening my point of view, I now confess publicly I hold for each immense admiration, appreciation, and affection for their contributions to Alaska.

Table of Contents

PART ONE
Close Encounters of the Absurd Kind

1 The Good and Bad Old Days........................14
2 Muscle Mania..21
3 Bear Facts—and Fancy..................................26
4 Bear Charges and Challenges.......................32
5 High-Flying Friends......................................36
6 People I Seem To Be....................................42
7 Floundering Amid Fins, Feathers, & Fur.....47
8 Survivor...52
9 Odd Encounters...59

PART TWO
Rocking the Ship of State

10 Stumbling Aboard......................................64
11 A Motley Crew...69

12 The Right Course............................76
13 Wild Waters..................................82
14 The Privateers...............................87
15 A New Upper Berth.........................93
16 High Winds..................................99
17 Treasures Unearthed.......................104
18 Shanghaied.................................110
19 Reluctant Reenlistment....................115
20 Captain and Crew..........................121

PART THREE
Burning Issues Still Smoldering

21 Ever Cry Wolf..............................130
22 Dividend Delusions.........................135
23 The Great Lands of Alaska.................142
24 More Knots to Untangle....................150

PART FOUR
Didn't You Used to Be Somebody?

25 Speaking Disengagements...................156
26 Campaign Capers............................162
27 Rough Running..............................168
28 The Golden Years? My Gluteus!.............174
29 Root of My Problems........................179
30 Touring the Twilight Zone..................186
    INDEX......................................191

Nephew David McRae and I use a cradle saw fashioned by master mechanic Mike Vandergrift.   1998

Foreword

Broadcaster Paul Harvey is known for telling "the rest of the story." This book is "the rest of the story" from Jay Hammond, Alaska's much-loved governor whose first book, *Tales of Alaska's Bush Rat Governor*, simply couldn't hold all his wonderful stories.

Hammond is reminiscent of Davy Crockett. Like Crockett, he is an expert woodsman who can recount numerous adventures with bears, wolves, and other critters, and he is a great political leader who rose to the top by popular acclaim. How could anyone be a more ideal Alaskan?

In self-deprecating anecdotes (no one laughs at Hammond more than Hammond), he takes readers along on his wilderness adventures as a hunting/fishing guide and bush pilot, his two terms as governor, and his dozen years as a legislator. Though his years as governor ended two decades ago, Hammond's voice continues to influence Alaska's course.

As a legislator Hammond gleefully twisted tails of his fellows and others with his publicly read doggerel, for which he has unlimited talent. A generous allotment of these verses are found herein, with the place they played in politics. The book also takes some satisfaction in revealing a few embarrassing historical facts about certain former legislators.

It has been my privilege to know Jay Hammond for half a century. His interest in others and their welfare is genuine. He has dedicated thirty years of his life to public service in Alaska. He is loyal to his friends, and he unhesitatingly backed his administration's appointees (I was one of them). He is deeply devout, but he doesn't wear religion on his sleeve. I once told him but for his honesty he could have become a great con man, for he has the amazing ability of solving seemingly unsolvable problems by probing at them in unexpected ways. This talent has served him well as a legislator, as governor, and as a respected elder statesman.

As governor, Hammond wrote his own speeches. He wrote his first book, and he penned every word of this one. His command of language, written and oral, is awesome. Hammond's new book—an intimate, humorous second look at the life of this former governor—should please all Alaskans, as well as others who are fascinated with the Alaskan way of life.

Jim Rearden

—————————— **Preface** ——————————

There's something insufferably presumptuous about an old has-been politician who writes an autobiography in the apparent belief anyone gives a tinker's damn about where he's been or what he's up to. Hence it came as a surprise when *Tales of Alaska's Bush Rat Governor* sold more than a handful of copies.

The answer has to be the indecent exposure the book received when Charley Gibson of *Good Morning America* held up a naked copy on camera and said: "I've not yet read your book, though I hear it's great. But tell me, what in the world is a bush rat?"

"I've always been afraid to ask," was my response. I went on to explain that *Bush Rat* was not my choice of title, but the one upon which the publisher insisted. (Maybe he had the right idea, since a bush rat is a person who leaves the Alaskan bush only upon enormous provocation and is permitted entree by the townspeople with even greater reluctance.)

"What was your title choice? "asked Charley.

I told him I had preferred two or three others. One related to an incident a year after I'd left office. I was out shopping when a young sales clerk kept glancing up furtively, no doubt wondering on which post office wall she had spotted my bearded visage. Finally, overcome with curiosity, she blurted: "Didn't you used to be somebody"?

I thought that would make a far better title than *Bush Rat*—just as I did of my first proposal, *Alaskan, Crude*, deemed by my publisher too confusing, and *Posy Sniffing Swine*, a label spanked on me by crusty old miner Joe Vogler, the rabidly anti-environmentalist leader of the Alaska Independence Party. It was not until long after Joe was gunned down by a would-be burglar that I learned the context in which he had used that wondrously flamboyant description. While testifying before a congressional committee against what he felt to be yet another outrageous incursion into Alaska by the federal government, he remarked: "Though Hammond may be a posy-sniffing swine, he at least didn't sell out the state to the oil companies." From Joe that was high praise.

Back when it was suggested I write *Bush Rat*, I wondered how long it should be? One thousand pages seemed ample. I ended up with fourteen hundred. My publisher wanted only four hundred. Consequently most of the manuscript ended up in my bulging round file. What is to be done with this great overlode, I asked myself. The answer lies in this fresh volume.

For this new book I panned through the overflowing detritus and sifted the nuggets from the clinkers. Among the finds were stories of cherished relationships, and of personal experiences both hilarious and harrowing from days of my youth and later as a pilot, a wilderness guide, and last and certainly least, a politician. In order to tell the truth about my days in the state capital, it even became necessary to resort to rhyme.

Additionally it seemed appropriate to at least sniff around some still-smoldering Alaskan issues, a couple of which were first kindled during my administration. Since to date such issues as subsistence hunting and the use of earnings from Alaska's Permanent Fund have defied quenching, I felt obligated to suggest means by which they could be extinguished.

Perhaps my major inducement to do a second book was the series of amazing experiences I encountered while touring the "twilight zone" between traditional and alternative medical practices. The public is largely unaware of the potentials and pitfalls of procedures that have had such profound impact upon me and a multitude of others, and I hope to open some eyes and minds to approaches that might alleviate suffering.

Since publication of *Bush Rat* in 1994, two women who provided encouragement and inspiration for that effort have gone to their reward. Both were beloved and are missed beyond measure by those privileged to have known them.

Kay Fanning, editor and savior of the *Anchorage Daily News* during my years in public office and later editor of the *Christian Science Monitor,* was one who exemplified in spades the expression "class act." A woman of unswerving dedication and devotion to those and that in which she believed, she was a slayer of dragons, many of whom later came to greatly respect her. Suzan Nightingale was a columnist of extraordinary talent who wrote for the *Daily News.* I came to appreciate her full capabilities during a two-week period of total editorial immersion when she spent a dozen hours a day helping to make sense of my scribblings for my first book.

I've learned to accept the fact that I am still afflicted with a grievous frailty all too common in politicians and bureaucrats: why use ten words when ten thousand will do? I once thought I was one of the good guys hurling rocks at the bureaucracy. Then it dawned on me that with four years in the Marine Corps, seven with the U.S. Fish and Wildlife Service, three as a mayor, twelve as a legislator, and eight as governor, I'm the biggest bureaucrat I know. That many people, myself included, do not recognize me as a *politician* is perhaps the greatest act of self-delusion, and public con job, I've ever pulled off. I'm constantly amazed at the kind and gracious treatment I'm accorded by Alaskans. Apparently many are either wondrously forgiving or forgetful. I can only hope for the same puzzling but pleasing response from readers of this new volume.

Bella and I at a banquet where I received the Walter J. Hickel award for Distinguished Public Policy Leadership in June, 2001. As per columnist Mike Doogan's advice, I brought a taste tester with me to the banquet. Both Bella and I survived.
Anchorage; Chuck Meachem photo

PART ONE

Close encounters of the absurd kind

1The good and bad old days

I was still looking a bit shell-shocked after a close encounter
with screen star Lana Turner at Laguna Beach.   1943

THERE'S NOTHING LIKE old age to awaken memories of youth and of the people who have since gone to their reward. Some memories are happy, some sad, some ridiculous, and some still conjure up nightmares. One of the latter—a true horror tale—relates to a canoe trip in the Adirondacks that I took at age fourteen with my close friend Robert Nichols. That our friendship endured my often corrupting his name to Rubber Nipples, or Nippy, was somewhat surprising. That it survived the following is downright amazing.

We had capsized the canoe and lost most supplies several days before reaching the village of Saranac Lake, where we had planned to resupply. To our surprise, we found that after the first few days without food we got rather used to not eating. Instead we steeped our stomachs in strong tea, which we had in abundance.

Curiously, what we both craved was ginger ale. While paddling to near exhaustion, the thought of soon consuming a bottle of ice-cold Canada Dry prompted a redoubling of effort. After almost a week we finally arrived at a small country store on the shore of Saranac Lake. Our first purchase was two quarts of ginger ale. On a bench alongside the store we each swilled a full quart—and got loop-legged drunk! After staggering around for awhile we passed out on the lawn and slept it off.

Perhaps Canada Dry back then was more potent. Or perhaps our condition was due to self-hypnosis. Years later I witnessed some primitive peoples reacting the same way when told the soda pop they were drinking was hard liquor.

Since Saranac is a large lake and the wind was up, we gladly accepted the offer of a wizened old codger to give us a lift while he towed our canoe behind his skiff to his cabin halfway down the lake. Leonard Horatio Austin was a cackling, happy-go-lucky old leprechaun whose degeneracy and lethal potential were initially obscured under a stream of nonstop merry chatter.

Coming alongside the dock to let us board, he was hailed from another boat by the local game warden: "Hey, Len, I suppose you've been out poaching bass again."

"You bet," joshed our new friend. "Got three dandies here in the well. Come on over and see 'em."

Fact is he really did have three illegal bass in the well; but apparently such was his reputation for prevarication no one believed him. So the warden merely snorted, shook his head, and sailed on.

Arriving at his tiny, decrepit log cabin, the old fellow leaped nimbly ashore and invited us in for a meal. Stowing our gear under the bunk beds adjoining our host's rude pallet, we offered to help with the evening repast. After a meal of mystery meat and gummy biscuits, Aussie, as he referred to himself, subjected us to a ceaseless stream of raunchy jokes and a trek down memory lane through a number of old photograph albums. That his memory lane proved more nightmare alley soon became apparent by the disturbing relish he took in exhibiting pictures dealing with death, mutilation, and pedophilia.

We were suddenly queasy about spending the night, but the storm raging outside, plus confidence in our combined abilities to subdue the wizened old gnome, made us decide to stay. I leaped into the top bunk as far from the master's bed as I could, leaving Nippy with the bottom bunk. After a few sleepless hours I finally dozed off. A shriek from below soon blew me awake and bolt upright. Beneath me I heard a frantic thrashing about, and from under tangled bedclothes shot a most distraught fourteen-year-old boy. Aussie had crawled in with Nip and tried to cuddle.

With that, we abandoned all pretense at further slumber. Having never undressed, we had but to gather our gear and flee. We hastily scurried about, but our gnarled host blocked the door, grinning evilly. "Come on, just try to get by me and see what happens," he cackled. "Come on. Or are ya skeered?"

Nip and I made a tentative move toward the old geezer. With that he lashed out with a scrawny arm and, as if by magic, in his fist appeared a saber-long butcher knife. Waving that under our noses, he chortled: "Suppose you got that away from me." He then threw the knife on the table, and from behind the door produced a lethal-looking hand axe. Giggling insanely, he twirled that about his head and invited us to try to take it from him.

Both Nip and I could do nothing but shrink back from this escapee of our worst nightmares. Delighted by our distress, our demented host flung the axe into the corner, capered to the closed door, and challenged us again to get past. For a moment I debated trying to charge through him. That debate was cut short when from behind a bit of canvas hung next to the door he produced an old hog-leg revolver. Its bore seemed wide enough for both Nip and me to crawl into.

After flourishing the cocked revolver, first under my nose, then Nip's, he giggled: "OK, you fellers can see you can't beat old Aussie, so mind what I tell ya. You try to escape and I'll track you down. I know these woods and waters better than anyone so you can't git away. Tomorrow I'm going down to the village and you better be here when I get back. If you ain't, I'll know you stole from me. Then I'll go find you and make you sorry. And if there's one thing old Aussie knows how to do, it's to make young boys sorry."

Nip and I spent the rest of the night cowering next to each other on a wooden bench. With daylight our crazed host prepared to leave by boat for the village. His last words were a repeat of his warning to stay put.

As soon as his skiff disappeared, Nip and I hustled gear and hind-quarters to our canoe and fled in the other direction. I doubt if the canoe even broke the lake's surface tension, so fast did we fly from Aussie's domain. We traveled well into the night before making camp under our canoe, deep in the woods, far from shore. Nonetheless, I don't think either of us slept for a moment. It was only after several miles and days later that we concluded we'd seen the last of the old derelict.

This misadventure was to prompt one of the most detestable things I've ever done. Though since regretted, at the time it gave me fiendish pleasure. A month or so after the escapade, Nip incurred my extreme displeasure for some reason long since forgotten. In retaliation, I mailed a note to Aussie, signed "Nip," inviting him to spend the Christmas holidays with the Nichols family. At the time, I relished the picture of the old lunatic arriving, carpetbag in hand, at the door of the horrified Nichols clan. But some shred of decency still feebly clinging obliged me to include the following caveat: "Since we may be visiting relatives elsewhere for the holidays, please let me know well in advance if you can make it."

When Nip received Aussie's letter eagerly accepting his "kind invitation," he was apoplectic. After hastily scrawling a note informing him the Nichols family would likely be in Timbuktu for the holidays, Nip called me and gave me a well-deserved blistering that even my tears of laughter did little to cool.

AT THE OPPOSITE END of memory lane lie thoughts of my father, the Reverend Morris Hammond, who died of Lou Gehrig's disease in 1956. After being diagnosed only a year or so earlier, his decline was precipitous. Though almost unable to walk and barely able to speak for six days of the week, amazingly on Sundays he could climb unaided to the pulpit in the Rupert, Vermont, Methodist church and deliver sermons with almost full vocal power. This he attributed to the Holy Spirit. While skeptics suggested that self-hypnosis or some other psychological quirk should be given the credit, years later I was given reason to believe my father had the right answer.

I'd been asked to speak one Sunday at an Anchorage church. The day before, I came down with a severe case of laryngitis, just prior to a scheduled speech to the Anchorage Chamber of Commerce. Once at the podium I could barely croak. Reading a note I'd scribbled, the emcee announced my predicament and told the crowd that I would be unable to give my speech. This prompted a standing ovation.   .

But now it was Sunday, and I hoped to provide a bit of testimony to the blessings I'd found when I crossed from the dark side of the street into the light of the Good Lord's saving grace. Just before awaking that morning, I had a vivid dream of my dad and the clarity of his speech, despite his illness, while giving his sermons. That dream was still on my mind when I was introduced to the preacher, Rev. Alonzo Patterson.

Hello, governor. How nice of you to come," he said. ""But where is your father? I understood he would be with you.

Somewhat stunned, I croaked in response: "No, I'm afraid not. He died several years ago."

After rising to try to give my testimonial, I was amazed to find I could speak normally. That amazement redoubled in spades when upon leaving the church I again lost my voice and could not speak without difficulty for the next several days. Self-hypnosis, religious hysteria, or psychosomatic effect? Perhaps it was one of those, though I believe otherwise. In light of entirely too many such occurrences, I find that "faith" in the dogma of *disbelief* requires a far broader leap than does acceptance of the Holy Spirit as an explanation.

DURING MY FATHER'S FINAL ILLNESS, my mother provided loving care leavened with a warm sense of humor that, though often taxed, helped ease family crises. I like to think my older brother Bill did more taxing than I ever did. For instance, there was the road trip during which Mother proposed we play a game. She challenged us with the question: "If you were on a desert island and could have but one food, what would it be?"

My wife, Bella, as I recall, said watermelon; Bill's wife, Eva, a devout Texan, probably said grits; I wanted lobster.

"What about you, Billy?" chirped Mother brightly.

"Why, mother's milk, of course, preferably from a rather young mother."

For a moment, stunned silence. Then as Mother's cheerful countenance collapsed in horror she gasped "How *rotten!*"—only to have her reproval fall flat when she burst into laughter, to which all chimed in save Billy, who smugly hid behind a straight face his delight in having once again shocked his audience.

RESURRECTING THE ERA of my youth and those who patrolled it can be a bit spooky, as I discovered when I returned to visit a farm in upstate New York where I had worked at age fourteen. In my book *Tales of Alaska's Bush Rat Governor,* I described the series of macabre, sometimes life-threatening events and characters I had encountered while working there. Most of the farmhands (save myself, of course) were derelicts or certifiably insane. One was an escaped con who, in exchange for backbreaking servitude, was being harbored by the sadistic farm owner. Perhaps most memorable was the earthy, red-haired gypsy woman who shared the squire's bed and board, totally oblivious that she kindled tinder beneath my simmering pubescent hormones along with resentment for the rough manner in which she was treated by Farmer Fred.

Even in 1936, the summer I worked there, the farmhouse seemed about to collapse. When I visited the site in 1985 with my daughter Heidi, the farm had gone to brush and appeared abandoned. Seven years later I returned with my wife, Bella, and my nephew David. It was a cold, gloomy day in March when we drove up to the farm, now virtually obscured from the main road by thick vegetation. Even the barns were now collapsing; the house was in worse shape. The porch had slumped into the weeds. No vestige of paint remained on the gray clapboard siding. Plywood covered a few broken windows like eye patches on a bleached skull.

Plowing our way through several inches of snow, we drove up the rutted dirt drive for a look. David and I got out of the car for a closer inspection of the house, which apparently had long since been abandoned. Suddenly we spotted tracks leading to the front door, but not emerging. The tracks seemed those of a pair of old-fashioned women's shoes, and they somehow appeared witchlike to our now spooked-up imaginations. What was going on here? Had some old derelict sought refuge from the weather and expired within? No smoke curled from the crumbling brick chimney and not a glint of light came from behind the few remaining grimy windowpanes.

Should we knock on the door, or try to force entry? There seemed something weirdly disquieting that kept us from doing either. The decrepit old building had all the chilling appeal of the Bates Motel of *Psycho* fame. David whispered: "If that door opens we're liable to have some shrieking apparition fly down the hall at us some three feet off the ground wielding a bloody hatchet." My thoughts precisely. So we two chickens flew back to our coop in the car and beat a hasty retreat.

Five years later my second cousin Barbara Wakefield, who lives in Saratoga, New York, enlightened us on the facts. It seems the gypsy girl had ultimately married Farmer Fred and continued to reside at the old farmstead after he left this world. At the time of our aborted visit, she had to be well into her nineties and long since retired from teaching school, where she had established a fine reputation and was greatly loved by her erstwhile students and the community. So much for my addition to ghost story anthology. Next they'll tell me Bigfoot and the Loch Ness Monster are also figments, not fact!

I WAS ALSO BROUGHT BACK to the time of my youth on the day I learned Lana Turner had died. Her voice was silenced forever in 1995, but I still remembered it clearly, though the last time I heard it was more than a half century past and the screen star was nothing more than a fleeting acquaintance.

I was strolling, head down, on the sands of Laguna Beach shortly before shipping out to the South Pacific with my squadron during World War II when that voice asked: "Do you have the time?" Looking up I was astonished to see Lana Turner and her small daughter Cheryl Crane lolling atop a beach blanket. Since clearly I was wearing no wristwatch and could not have inserted a quarter into the pocket of my tight swimming trunks, much less a pocket watch, I thought the question somewhat odd. However, overawed by Lana's fame and furbishing, I stifled my inclination to respond with some smart-alecky remark like "Time for what?"

Instead we chatted for a few minutes. Admittedly she did most of the talking while I grunted responses and did my best to concentrate on the conversation rather than her construction. It was not easy. The three strategically placed doilies adorning her fuselage left no question as to why she had earned the sobriquet Sweater Girl.

However, so warm and friendly was she that my tongue slowly started unknotting to where I might have even asked her for a date had not a huge stretch limo then driven up to the stairs that led down to the beach. There it disgorged four Hollywood types, including the latest of what would become a total of six husbands: her recently divorced spouse Steve Crane. All four made it abundantly clear my presence was no longer required, so rather than continuing to soar some three feet above ground, I slunk off to plunge into the cooling surf, shucking whatever warm fantasies had climbed aboard.

2 Muscle mania

This picture in the *Pittsburgh Post Gazette* brought me a
number of mash notes. Two were from women.
Pennsylvania State College, 1941; Gene Wettstone photo

I STARTED WEIGHT LIFTING in the early 1940s, back when it was considered—and perhaps was—a pursuit of oddballs. But well before I turned from weight lifting to politicking—truly an oddball pursuit—the activity became not only popular but virtually compulsory for athletes. Through it I met many memorable characters.

One such was the indestructible Dr. John Ziegler, who achieved an incredible degree of self-rehabilitation against overwhelming odds. I first met John in 1970 while visiting some old weight-lifting friends at the York Barbell company in Pennsylvania. A barrel-chested behemoth, at six-foot-four weighing about 250 pounds, he was an imposing figure. Assigned a few years before as doctor to the U.S. Olympic weight-lifting team, which then held many world titles, John had developed some extraordinary training techniques. One was an electronic exercise device that required no conscious effort to use. Pads were attached to the athlete and then a rheostat was turned up to send electrical impulses to various muscle groups. At high voltage, a half hour's use was equal to three hours of pumping iron. The winner of that year's Mr. America bodybuilding competition attributed his success primarily to Ziegler's device. After an exhausting half hour exposed to its tender mercies, I felt I'd been stomped on by a team of Clydesdales.

John Ziegler's most remarkable accomplishment was his recuperation from what should have been terminal injuries. As an Army sergeant in the Pacific during World War II, he and his squad were attacked by the Japanese and all save Ziegler were killed by machine-gun fire. Severely wounded and writhing in pain, he was bayoneted through the chest. Ziegler continued to twitch, so an officer put a Nambu handgun to his head and fired a shot into his brain.

When U.S. forces quickly overran the Japanese, they found Ziegler still breathing. Next came months of hospitalization and the prognosis that he would spend the rest of his days as a vegetable confined to a wheelchair. Instead he was to rehabilitate himself in a most remarkable manner. Though weight training at that time was frowned on by most doctors, through such training Ziegler slowly went from skeletal apparition to ambulatory, robust health. Even more amazing was his recapture of brain function and memory. That Japanese bullet, instead of totally scrambling his gray matter, seemed to open up new pathways to genius.

Only an average student prior to the war, Ziegler now flashed through medical school and was awarded a teaching chair at Johns Hopkins University, in Baltimore. His newfound genius was not without blemish, however. While he quickly built up a thriving medical practice, his colleagues and nurses found him irresponsible when it came to keeping appointments. Despite a full calendar, Ziegler, an ardent history buff, would take off without notice to engage in reenactments of action at Gettysburg or the Little Big Horn.

I witnessed some of Ziegler's eccentricities when I accompanied him on a wild ride from York to Washington, D.C. Careening along at over 120 miles an hour, the good doctor expounded nonstop with brilliant exuberance on every subject one could imagine, such as the brain-bombing impact of the newly discovered psychedelic LSD, which I suspect he was on. As he rambled verbally all over the landscape, I feared he would do so physically as well, since he sometimes gesticulated with both hands, while I in my distress desperately clutched the seat with both hands and hindquarters. It was abundantly clear that Ziegler occupied another dimension than most of us earthlings.

I suppose that after what he had been through in life, Ziegler thought he was immortal. Unwilling to challenge that assumption further, I declined his offer of a return ride to York and took the bus.

While in York I revisited a boyhood idol, John Grimek—winner of the first Mr. America bodybuilding title and also deemed by muscle man Arnold Schwarzenegger to be his hero. Grimek attributed his own remarkable physique to weight training, which prior to World War II had been scoffed at by most doctors and coaches. They claimed it bound muscles and enlarged the heart. My visit with Grimek awakened memories of my days as a student at Pennsylvania State College in 1940, where I was the only football player to use weights. I was joined in this pursuit by no more than half a dozen other students, including three gymnasts.

The coach of the Penn State gymnasts, Gene Wettstone, who later went on to coach the U.S Olympic gymnastic team, was adamantly opposed to any of his athletes pumping iron. Therefore we were surprised when he accepted our challenge to accompany us to the annual birthday party of Bob Hoffman, editor of *Strength and Health* magazine, then the bible of the weight-lifting fraternity. In those days, Hoffman and his stable of lifters dominated the weight-lifting world. Despite relative U.S. apathy, they had captured several international titles, including some from the Soviet Union. At the birthday party, lifters and bodybuilders competed. Before competition began, we took Coach Wettstone with us to visit the locker room, where the muscle men were suiting up—or rather, down.

One incredible specimen caught Wettstone's eye. At about five-foot-eight and 230 rock-hard pounds, John Grimek was an eye-popping exhibit. Arms with twenty-inch biceps hung from a huge torso suspended above a tiny waist that virtually matched the thirty-two-inch circumference of thighs like tree trunks.

"Impressive, yes," agreed Wettstone. " But I'll bet with all that bulk you have trouble bending over to touch your toes."

"You know, you're right," Grimek said. "Though I think I might still manage, just barely."

With a groan he bent from the waist and, bouncing a time or two, was indeed just barely able to touch his toes—with his *elbows!* Later demonstrations of one-arm chinning while holding a heavy dumbbell in his other hand plus a series of smoothly executed forward and back flips made Wettstone's jaw drop—along with his anti-weight training bias. We returned to Penn State with fifteen hundred pounds of new iron and a gym coach dedicated to preaching the gospel of weight training.

It's a gospel that has since spread far and wide, with most coaches and doctors now holding a favorable view. That I should indulge in weight training while it was still being denigrated is but another example of my being on the wrong side of attitudes popular at the moment—a circumstance often to haunt me later in political life.

AT PENN STATE, some of my weight-lifting colleagues and I formed an acrobatic dance group that gained much attention. One act had me prone on the floor while a female member of the group laid down on my extended arm. I would then slowly stand and press her up and down a few times with the one arm before hurling her to a partner. While simpler than it looked, since the lady weighed only about 100 pounds and in those days I could one-arm press 150, the act impressed the crowd. A picture of me performing this modest feat was featured in the *Pittsburgh Post Gazette* and elicited all manner of phone calls and mash notes. Two were from women.

While I since have known many admirable homosexuals, back then most heterosexuals viewed them as virtual lepers. Accordingly, none of the mash notes were answered and phone calls were quickly truncated. Nonetheless, one inadvertent contact was to cause me to flunk my first Navy flight physical.

A handsome young fellow named Robbie often watched our acrobatic dance team practice. I assumed he came to observe the scantily clad female members. Later I learned of his orientation—and that I was the object of his interest. Upon this startling revelation I let it be known that he had best keep his distance. Some weeks later, not long after the Japanese attack on Pearl Harbor, a Navy recruiting team came to Penn State, hoping to put together a squadron of students to go through flight training and into combat together. I and several other students decided to take the physical exam. I already had my private pilot's license, obtained under the government's civilian pilot training program, which required that in a national emergency I enlist in the Army, Navy, or Marine air arm.

Inside the examination building, applicants moved down an assembly line of chairs placed in the corridor. When it came my turn to enter the examination room, I left my seat in front of the door, walked into the room, and was asked to remove all clothing. As I did so I heard a scuffle outside in the hallway and looked up to see Robbie seated in my vacated chair, hot eyes riveted to my body. Slamming the door I slumped, seething, onto the examination table just as the doctor arrived to take my pulse and blood pressure. Both had jumped off the charts. I failed miserably.

After explaining the circumstances to a sympathetic recruiting officer, he advised that if I wished to take the test again, I could do so in Philadelphia. Two weeks later in that city I handily passed the physical.

IN THE LATE 1940S, while attending the University of Alaska at Fairbanks, I engaged once more in an acrobatic hand-balancing act. My partners, Freddie Fleck and Gloria Wassermen, had ridden bicycles up from New York, where Freddie had performed a hand-balancing routine at a small carnival. At only 140 pounds, he was a superb top man. Gloria, however, proved the major attraction. A beautiful, abundantly endowed, sloe-eyed brunette, her 120 pounds were most appropriately distributed over her five-foot, six inches. While totally feminine, she was incredibly strong. Often while we worked out, some macho type would stride up and, hoping to impress her, try to press a barbell that weighed about the same as Gloria. When he could not, Gloria delighted in grabbing the bar and doing a few repetitions.

Weighing in at 210, I of course was bottom man for the act. At least we started that way. One day, however, we were trying a new routine that Gloria, as the person in the middle, could not quite master.

"Here, let me bottom-stand and you show me how I should do it, " she instructed me. After changing places, I was impressed with the rock-solid base she provided.

So was Freddie. "Say, do you think you can hold it if I do a top stand on Jay?"

"Sure," she said. "Go ahead."

With that, while she held me in the proper position, Freddie pressed up into a handstand from her wrists. Again, rock solid! Whereupon we promptly changed our entire routine as we performed at various night spots and service clubs for a few dollars and a free meal. Whenever we came out to perform, the crowd's assumption of course was that I, the Big Stoop, would anchor the wiry lad and the gorgeous girl. Instead, much to the audience's surprise and delight, Gloria did all the bottom chores, with me in the middle while Freddie cavorted about handstanding on high.

3 Bear facts... and fancy

Luke, Lucky, and Usook spoil Bella by pretending they like her sour-dough hotcakes—a Sunday morning ritual at our Lake Clark home.
Lake Clark, 1999; Jay Hammond photo

WHEN I WAS STILL NEW to Alaska, it wasn't long before my presumed knowledge of all things Alaskan outstripped my experience. For example, after a year I could, with assurance, tell you the difference between a brown bear and a grizzly bear—to say nothing of the difference between a Republican and a Democrat. Both such distinctions have since blurred. Conclusions once engraved in stone turned later to rubble. Take bears: In the mid-1940s when I came to Alaska, most biologists thought there were several subspecies of brown bears, and significant differences between these brown bears and grizzlies. I once read a learned treatise laying these out. *Ursus kidderai, Ursus guyas, Ursus middendorfi,* and so forth were described in exhaustive detail. Then followed an in-depth analysis of the taxonomic distinctions between brown and grizzly bears. The writer concluded that a major distinction was—now follow this closely—"the former lacked the sulcate crown found on the second pre-molar of the latter." This struck me as a little much. After all, territories of browns and grizzlies often overlap. Somehow I could not quite imagine a brown bear boar bent on amorous dalliance taking time to check the dentures of some prospective ladylove.

Most biologists later abandoned such means of telling the big bears apart. Once they had concluded major differences were due simply to diet, they tried to discard the term *brown bear* and designate all big bears as either *upland grizzlies* or *coastal grizzlies.* But the term *Alaskan brown bear,* deeply mired in romance and history, would not discard easily. Consequently, biologists for a while proposed that bears inhabiting Kodiak Island and the Bering Sea drainage were brown bears, and that all others were grizzlies. This course left some bears subject to having their forequarters termed brown and their hindquarters grizzly, should they stand astride the watershed.

Somewhat better, perhaps, was the later designation of *brown bear* for those members of *Ursus arctos* found within fifty miles of saltwater and of *grizzly* for those members found farther inland. The trouble is that I've often seen what one would call a classic, humpbacked, silver-tipped grizzly munching salmon at tidewater, and witnessed an archetype brown bear scrabbling for ground squirrels a hundred miles inland. Hence, pardon me if I must confess I can no longer tell you the difference. The same goes for distinguishing a Republican from a Democrat. Nowadays without a scorecard it's hard to tell them apart. Members of both parties span the spectrum between ultraconservative and ultraliberal. Perhaps in the case of politicians, examination of dentures may be as good as any means of identification.

As for the brown/grizzly bears, it appears that what distinctions there may be, at least in personality, are a result of diet. Understandable. A huge beast like the inland grizzly that is obliged to grub for the sparse living found in the hinterlands is more likely to have a mad-on for mankind's intrusions than does one belly-deep in fat salmon down by the coast. During most encounters with man, the typical coastal brown bear is comparatively placid. But don't count on it.

Most folks when they first take to the outback of Alaska do so with rifles held at high port, expecting the brush to erupt with a haired-out H-bomb at any moment. Then after witnessing the typical "charge" being 180 degrees away, they become far less cautious. The third, more sensible stage of behavior is arrived at by those who have experienced the "exhilaration" of a true bear charge: bet against it happening, but cover that bet with a hole card of no less than .30 caliber.

GRIZZLIES AND THE OCCASIONAL BLACK BEAR often stroll through our yard at Miller Creek on Lake Clark. Fortunately the creek has no spawning salmon to delay them so they simply pass through discreetly, inclined to shun our presence more than we theirs. Occasionally confrontations are comical, like the time a young black bear pressed his nose to our window and fled in mortal terror from his own reflection. Some encounters, however, prompt rapt attention. Two young grizzlies once "treed" me atop a fuel tank I was installing and kept me there for almost an hour.

During a recent fall, seven bears came through our place in a single day. And on one spring day, Bella had a close encounter that could have been lethal. With one of our four dogs at her heels, she had approached the gate in the pole fence surrounding our garden. As she swung it open, she almost clouted a keg-size hairy head that was on the far side of the gate, a mere five feet away in deep grass. More alarming was the presence of the two cubs flanking their mother.

The sow lurched to her feet and took one lunging step forward. Bella, though armed with nothing but a short garden dibble, claims she was less scared than surprised and responded with a strident: "Get outta here!" Properly cowed, the bear did precisely that, swatting her kids in a beeline before her.

Unfortunately not all such encounters end so fortuitously. At least a dozen of my acquaintances have survived bear attacks. Four others did not. One was dragged from his tent to his death by a Siberian brown bear. One was killed and consumed by a black bear. Another was killed while imprudently prodding a bear from its den with a pole, and the fourth met his death after startling a bear while it was feeding on a moose kill.

Most people who live to tell of a violent bear encounter wear a singular badge of evidence: they were at least partially scalped. Perhaps some atavistic urge prompts a bear to go for the hair as resembling most a feature common to the creatures it knows. Certainly almost every bear attack victim has had his or her hairdo dramatically altered.

Current opinion has it that if you are attacked by a black bear, you should fight back as hard as possible. By contrast, if attacked by a brown or grizzly, you should cover your head with your arms and roll into a fetal position. An attack in which this counsel was ignored occurred in the 1960s just up the road from where we then lived in Naknek. Our friends Dick Jensen and wife Charlotte had been upriver netting salmon. Their outboard motor failed, and they were caught by ebbing tide and left stranded. Their choice was either to spend a mosquito-plagued night in the skiff or walk to Naknek down five miles of road in the dark. They chose the latter despite the presence of several brown bears making nightly pilgrimages to village canneries to feed on garbage and salmon offal. Dick, as an accomplished big-game guide, knew the need for caution, but he was also aware that during salmon season most brown bears are well fed and quite docile.

Wading to shore, he and Charlotte fumbled their way up the bank to the road. About a quarter-mile up the road from our house they were but slightly startled to see what they thought was a dog dash in front of them and disappear in the brush to their left. However, upon hearing a clatter off to their right and spotting a large silhouette astride a trash barrel, they realized they had gotten between a brown bear sow and its cub. Dick shouted at Charlotte to run to the nearest cabin while he tried to distract the bear, which was now charging. He succeeded. The bear hit him like a linebacker and walloped him into a ditch. Rather than rolling into a ball and playing dead, Dick launched himself at the beast, pounding, shouting, and kicking. Knowing him, I've no doubt that he was more furious than frightened.

Thereafter followed moments of horror later attested to by Dick's injuries. His scalp and one ear were nearly detached. Bite and claw marks mutilated his shoulder. His face was an unrecognizable pulp, and one bite had severed his windpipe. Meanwhile Charlotte frantically pounded on the door of the small cabin owned by the Ivanoffs, but occupied at the time only by two of their children. At first the kids refused to open the door, believing a drunken brawl was taking place. Finally they let her in, and a few moments later from out of the gloom came a ghastly apparition. Dick staggered through the door, scalp flapping, face hamburger, clothes drenched in blood.

Borrowing a truck, Charlotte rushed Dick to a cannery doctor, who kept Dick from drowning in his own blood. Then came an emergency flight to Anchorage. After several hours on the operating table Dick was pretty well patched-up externally, though his head for weeks looked like a stitched baseball and he talked like Marlon Brando in *The Godfather*. Some people who knew him before the attack felt that scars from the conflict for a time puckered his personality and affected their relationship with him. If true, that's understandable. No one can do battle with a lumbering nightmare of such proportions and emerge with spirit unscathed. A lesser man would not have emerged at all.

DURING MY SEVEN YEARS as a professional government hunter I got an overfill of killing. One assignment, for example, required me to kill more than a dozen caribou four times a year to test them for cesium and strontium fallout from Soviet nuclear blasts in the Wrangell Islands. For a time it was feared that accumulations of radioactive poisons in the lichens upon which caribou feed might endanger people who ate caribou meat. Another assignment required me to shoot scores of imported blue foxes on Amchitka Island that were thought to have caused a decline in Aleutian geese.

I pretty much hung up my guns long ago and have small zest for hunting, though the frequent presence of bears on our property suggests the wisdom of having firearms handy. Fortunately it's been several years since I've had to shoot one. However, while guiding bear hunters I have had occasion to witness the incredible tenacity with which bears cling to life and the hazards a wounded one can impose. Never was this more evident than during the time many years ago when I guided our good friends Lucy McConnaughey and her husband, Mack, on a two-week hunt.

On our first day out, Lucy wounded a Dall ram that, after she emptied her rifle, was about to disappear over a ridge. So I shot it. While not faulting me, Lucy pleaded with me not to shoot her bear should she wound one, save as a last resort. "I want to kill that bear all by myself," she told me. Reluctantly I agreed to save *my* hide, if not hers.

A few days later, we spotted a brown bear approaching a few hundred yards up the beach. "Piece of cake," I said. "We'll just wait here and let him walk up your gun barrel." Lucy was a crack shot completely familiar with her heavy rifle, so I felt she would have no trouble dumping the bear in its tracks as it emerged between two sand dunes at about fifty yards. Suddenly something alerted it. Rising on its hind legs, it sniffed the breeze and presented Lucy with a perfect target. Taking aim, she touched off a round, hit the bear in the chest, and dropped it instantly in its tracks. Yet almost immediately it leaped to its feet and dashed toward a high bank, its enthusiasm for escape bolstered by a fusillade from Lucy's rifle.

Normally, just before it topped the rise I would have shot, because few things curdle my craw like a wounded animal. However, with her admonition not to shoot unless absolutely necessary firmly in mind, I resisted doing so, hoping Lucy's last shot had done its business. No such luck. Clambering up the steep bank, we noted to our dismay the bear already more than two hundred yards off, galloping through swamp water to the safety of some willows beyond. Once again Lucy emptied her rifle, and then told Mack and me to try to drop the bear before it gained cover. I placed the sights of my .338 at least two feet above the fleeing beast and fired. The round splashed water a good hundred yards short. Knowing it to be a waste of ammunition, I nonetheless raised my sights higher and fired again. To our surprise the bear skidded to earth and lay thrashing.

Wishing to put it out of its misery as quickly as possible, we floundered within closer range. "Look," I told Lucy, "it's still kicking so use as many rounds as necessary to put out his lights." Moving up to within about a hundred feet, Lucy fired again as I covered the pathetically still-kicking beast with my rifle, barely able to suppress the urge to fire. Twice more Lucy shot. Both rounds hit the chest cavity and should have been lethal. Yet at the second shot, the bear attempted to rise. I pleaded with Lucy, "Shoot him again, he's still twitching." She needed no urging. Now less than fifty feet from the poor brute she fired another round into its engine compartment. Incredibly the bear leaped to its feet and, jaws popping, came at us like an express train.

"Shoot him, Jay"! Lucy screeched while attempting to jack another shell into the chamber. By the time she hollered, I probably had already shot. We barely had time to leap aside as the bear crashed to the ground between us. This time there was not a quiver.

After skinning the animal we performed a rough autopsy. Of the eight bullets striking home, only my first shot, which had entered the right ham, might not have been lethal. The heart and lungs were virtually shredded. The spinal cord was almost severed, perhaps preventing the bear's brain from getting the message that it was really dead.

4 Bear charges and challenges

Bears sometimes act like our "yard" at Lake Clark
is their home, too. 1999; David McRae photo

BOB "SEA OTTER" JONES was a legend among peers for such exploits as sailing through Amchitka Pass in an open dory or playfully clapping brown bears on the rump while frolicking with them on the tundra. Bob is another old friend who, though having gone down that final trail, leaves a footprint or two in memory's turf. I can attest to some of the stories about him, having logged a bit of Aleutian dory time with Bob and joining him on bear-marking excursions.

In the days before the use of tranquilizers and other techniques for getting close enough to mark bears to help determine their habitats and range, our clumsy identity method was far more exhilarating. Sea Otter and I, along with Bill Golly, a remarkably agile Aleut lad, would try to get above a bear on a streambed so we could douse it from the bank with a bucket of International Orange paint. Having been able to mark only a few bears in this manner, we were pleased when one morning we found two brown bears on the beach slowly moving up a steep hill. Climbing as fast as we could to the top, we peered over the side, only to find ourselves nearly nose to nose with both bears en route upward.

Bob and I decided to take some close-up pictures. Bill stood by, supplied with a fistful of Roman candles and a glowing cigar butt to light them if we needed to scare off the bears. At first the bears obliged us in our photo plans, lying in tandem just a few feet away. Bob had his Speed Graphic. I had a 16mm movie camera. As the bears placidly chewed their cud and peered at us myopically through inscrutable boar-hog eyes, we set up our cameras. But just as I started to grind away, my viewfinder suddenly filled with nothing but hair as the lead bear lunged toward us. Perched on the brink of the hill as I was, my escape route was obvious. Camera still grinding away, I sailed over the side. Sea Otter, however, was not about to accept the bear's advances unchallenged. Furious with it for disputing his claim that brown bears almost never charge with intent to maim, but simply run as a bluff, Bob executed a superb bull-ring Veronica and, as the bear barreled by, swiped its head with his heavy Speed Graphic. All this was accompanied by a stream of profanity fit to make a bosun blush.

Meanwhile, Bill frantically applied his glowing cigar butt to a whole clutch of Roman candles. Suddenly, rocketing great balls of fire accompanied the shower of verbal abuse hurled at the charging bear. Small wonder that both bears turned tail and fled. I'd not be surprised if they're *still* running!

Unfortunately the only feature of this ludicrous caper I captured on film was the lead brown bear crouching down; then nothing but hair, followed by a pinwheeling panorama of sea, sky, and sand as I catapulted over the bank.

NO ONE LIVED among bears more casually than did Howie Bass. Though his remains were never found, he may well have been a victim of this fact.

Howie's desire to record everything about brown bears compelled him to forsake the corporate comforts of a position within his family's business back East to indulge his passion. The best available movie equipment and mounds of film accompanied him whenever he had me fly him to my bear camp on Becharof Lake on the Alaska Peninsula.

At six-foot-four and 235 pounds, Howie was a gentle giant. With shoulder-length hair and spaced-out smile he seemed a classic flower child of the sixties. Disenchanted with the establishment, he wished to hole up in the wilds to commune with nature while he read the works of Carlos Castenada and other Age of Aquarius scribes.

Over the next few years Howie spent a total of several months on Becharof Lake, filming and recording an incredible catalog of brown bear activity. During that time I came to know him fairly well, though often he soared about at a heady altitude to which I'd not been given clearance. Clearly he felt greater kindred to all wild creatures than to humankind. That such intimacy might prove hazardous gave him no pause at all. When, for example, I suggested he exercise caution before picking up and fondling a bear cub in its mother's presence, he seemed surprised that I'd be concerned. "If I should be dispatched by a brown bear," he said, "I'd not mind at all. I can think of no more appropriate way to go than in total harmony with my karma and Mother Nature."

I've no doubt he meant it. Certainly he ignored even the most basic precautions. I once saw him advance, microphone at high port, between two battling brown bears, ducking adroitly between their clubbing claws to record several moments of primal battle.

I received a letter one day from a private investigator, who said he had been hired by Howie's family to ferret out information regarding their son's disappearance. "Since he was last reported to be at your Becharof Lake hunting camp, perhaps you have some information."

While I suspect some accommodating brown bear sent Howie to his reward, "in total harmony" with his "karma and Mother Nature," there are other possibilities. Howie's area of operations overlapped those of Billy Nekeferoff, an infamous psychotic multi-murderer who had burned out three guide camps in the area. No doubt he resented Howie's intrusion into his domain. Perchance they crossed trails and dispatched one another, since both disappeared at the same time. It's also quite possible Billy or Howie or both perished by falling through the ice, which on Alaska Peninsula lakes can be treacherous.

WHILE MOST of my departed old friends had exceeded their allotted three score years and ten, Michio Hoshino's total was cut tragically almost in half, stunning all who had come to know and love him. Bella and I first met Michio long before he gained fame as a wildlife photographer. For his splendid work he later was proclaimed by the Japanese government to be that nation's number one photographer. His superb, distinctive style is evident in such award-winning volumes as *Grizzly*, for which I was privileged to do the foreword.

Michio had been sent to our place on Lake Clark to take some photos to accompany an article on us to be published in the *Tokyo Times*. During the three days he spent here, he almost shattered the complacent and chauvinistic domestic tranquility I'd been enjoying for over thirty years. Although when Bella and I were first married I did much of the cooking, over time I'd ceased doing so and had pretty well conned Bella into assuming that chore as the wife's role. This she has done expertly since, with rare complaint. When Michio arrived with ample foodstuff to feed all and insisted on doing the cooking, which he did superbly, I knew I was in trouble. Talk about alienation of affections! Another few days and I believe Bella would have nailed Michio to the floor to keep him from leaving and taken me out to the dump.

In subsequent years Michio and I crossed trails on all too few occasions. Each encounter served to further both my esteem and affection for this remarkable man. When Michio asked if he and his soon-to-be bride might honeymoon at our place, we were delighted: Bella perhaps in anticipation of someone sharing the cooking; I in relief that my wife would not likely run off with a newly married man, despite his far greater virtues. Unfortunately, circumstances resulted in these honeymoon plans being changed. Michio did marry, however, and he fathered two children. But he was to die much too soon, shortly before the birth of his second child.

In 1996, Michio accompanied a group of Russian scientists studying Siberian brown bears on a remote stream teeming with salmon. There they set up camp while Michio set up his cameras. The small cabin used for sleeping was crowded, and Michio elected to sleep in his tent. During the night his screams alerted the others who, rushing out, saw a bear hauling his thrashing body into the brush. By the time they were able to drive the bear off, Michio had expired.

That such a tragedy should befall one so experienced around dangerous game raised several questions. Normally bears that have gorged on salmon are rather passive and avoid human contact. One explanation was that the rogue bear may have been injured. Possibly it was the same oddly behaving bear that had prompted one member of the expedition to scramble atop the cabin roof a short time before.

Eschewing firearms, the group had relied on pepper spray for bear repellent. While this can be effective at very short range, so long as the wind is at your back, used improperly it can instead *attract* bears. Some people believe the Russians had doused the skirts of Michio's tent with pepper spray, intending to ward bears off. Instead it could have been a magnet. Whatever the truth, though the tragedy took Michio's life much too soon, it served to increase the light and warmth of memories ensconced by Michio in the minds and hearts of all those enriched by having known him.

5 High-flying friends

Mike Vaandergrift astride his homebuilt minature tractor.
1963; Jay Hammond photo

AS A LONGTIME PILOT in a state that depends on air services, It's not surprising that many of the most memorable people I've met have been pilots. Who could ever forget Babe Alsworth, a pioneer bush pilot from Lake Clark who was the protagonist of any number of colorful stories—such as those about his methods of flight instruction, which compelled students to learn in remarkably short order if they were to survive. My brother-in-law Sam McRae told of having Babe teach him to fly by taking him up in his ski-equipped Taylorcraft, spending about an hour showing him some of the basics, then landing and telling Sam: "Go ahead. Take it up."

Not knowing any better, Sam taxied about on the ice for a few minutes, going a bit faster each circuit. Finally he added enough throttle to take off, flew around for a few minutes, and then landed with himself and the aircraft intact. He'd soloed after but one hour's instruction!

Babe's son Glen attests to Babe's laid back approach. "I was a late bloomer," Glen said. "My brothers all soloed by the time they were twelve. It took me until I was fourteen. Nonetheless I learned very quickly simply because I had to. Dad would remove his set of controls and you were instantly command pilot, like it or not."

In his late eighties Babe was still instructing his grandkids, though it's questionable whether he was licensed to do so. This lack of official sanction, however, would have given him no pause whatsoever. Babe was pretty casual when it came to compliance with government regulations. This of course drove agencies such as the IRS and FAA to distraction—precisely what Babe had in mind. Once in a televised interview I asked him: "Babe, I've known you for more than forty years and I've never heard of you busting an aircraft." At this he grinned and confessed that he "just never reported them," obviously relishing the memory of having put yet another fast one over on a government agency.

Rumor had it that Babe did his banking beneath his mattress. Certainly he hoarded gold so long as I knew him. For this, as for most temporal riches, Babe had only casual interest. John Claus tells of visiting Babe at the farmstead in Hawaii to which he retired. John noted a gaudy gilded brick being used as a doorstop. Thinking it odd that one would gold-paint a brick for such a mundane purpose, John thought it odder still when he picked it up for closer inspection and learned that it was solid gold! In another instance, Babe paid for a new Cessna 180 with sixteen thousand silver dollars. But Babe's greatest treasure by far was his wife, Mary.

A most remarkable woman, daughter of an Aleut mother and Scandinavian father, Mary was raised in the small Bering Sea fishing village of Pilot Point and there met Babe, who was flying for a local cannery. They married and moved to Lake Clark, where I met them in the mid-1940s. My introduction to Mary was not fortuitous. I'd flown game warden Bob Mahaffey into the newly constructed dirt strip at what is now Port Alsworth.

Taxiing back to a small cluster of cabins, I thoughtlessly gunned the engine while turning around and smothered Mary's line of freshly hung laundry with a billowing cloud of dust. From out of that cloud stormed an irate figure fulminating at me in both English and Aleut. While the latter was incomprehensible, her turn of phrase left no confusion as to just what Mary thought of my ancestry or where I likely would spend eternity. During several later encounters with Mary, even though I tiptoed about on my best behavior as though walking on eggs, I still somehow often managed to insert my yolk-begrimed foot in my mouth. Mary did not suffer fools kindly. Yet suddenly her attitude underwent remarkable change.

One day a few years after our first confrontation, I was enthralled to find a brand new Mary Alsworth. She had ceased smoking and cussing; she was now more soothing stream than pent-up volcano. What a transformation! Her hospitality was unbounded, her counsel wise and appreciated. As time went on, I learned that Mary could do more things well than most anyone I've ever known. She acted as weather observer, radio operator, postmistress, home schoolteacher, wife, and mother to five uniquely accomplished children. While in those days Port Alsworth had no school, Mary made sure her kids got an education. Though her oldest, Lonnie, was killed in a tragic plane accident, the others have all done exceedingly well in their chosen fields. People like Mary Alsworth inspired by example and enriched the lives of all who knew her.

Mary's metamorphosis from berating harridan to benevolent hostess was attributable to her religious conversion. It is but one of innumerable instances where I've seen the momentous change that takes place when one not only accepts but practices the teachings of Christ. It's enough to break through the crust of the most calloused skeptic. Mary, like most true Christians, expressed her faith more through example than through preaching or censure.

Babe likewise got religion, which he was determined to share with one and all no matter how uninvited. Old friend Dick Proeneke was among the targets for Babe's messianic missiles. Dick, for some twenty years our nearest neighbor to the north, was co-author of *One Man's Wilderness*, a chronicle of life in a small, meticulously self-built cabin on Twin Lakes, deep in the Alaska Range. When Babe first flew Dick to Twin Lakes and deposited him on shore, Dick gazed about at the majestic scenery and remarked to Babe: "This must be heaven."

"Huh!" the crusty old bush pilot scoffed: "This is a dung heap compared to heaven."

Babe was noted for pithy responses that often set folks back on their heels. So it was that shortly after Babe became religious he confessed to a couple of village missionary ladies that despite his desire to clean up his act, he still enjoyed an occasional glass of wine.

"Oh my," was their startled response, "that has to go. Tell you what, next time you feel the urge to drink wine, take a laxative."

Babe complied; when the drinking urge again came upon him, he took some Ex-Lax. When queried about its effectiveness by the missionary ladies, Babe confessed it had done nothing to quench his thirst. They counseled a new approach: "Since that didn't work, next time you have the urge to drink a glass of wine, take an enema."

"Well," Babe was alleged to have responded, "in the event of the Good Lord's second coming, I don't know whether I'd rather be caught clutching a glass of wine or an enema tube."

Babe's effort to forgo wine reminds me of the experience of my Naknek neighbor Vic Monsen. Vic, an enthusiastic imbiber of spirits, lived well into his eighties. Toward the end, in recognition of a need for moderation, Vic sought counsel from preacher Curtis Nestegard, who sensed a possible candidate for salvation if he could persuade Vic to allow Christ to help him quit drinking.

"Vic, if you'll just ask Him, Jesus will completely deliver you from that burden."

Pondering that for a moment, Vic said a bit wistfully: "Gee, Nestegard, *completely* isn't exactly what I had in mind." Vic, ever solicitous, apparently had no desire to overburden the Lord.

Vic also confessed to me a remarkable skill he had learned from some Laplanders who came to Naknek in the 1930s to teach reindeer husbandry to local herders. From them, Vic learned to neuter bull calves by biting off their testes. With this revelation I presented Vic with a shingle that read: "Dr. Molars Monsen. Oral Surgeon." He modestly declined to hang it out, declaring himself long out of practice.

MIKE VANDERGRIFT is a long-departed friend who could perform magic in repairing airplanes and virtually any other mechanical contrivance. Mike had come to Alaska in the early 1940s to work for Babe Alsworth. Acknowledged as a mechanical genius by all who knew him, Mike could cobble together from spit, string, wire, and tape the most complicated machines. I still have as a prized example of his extraordinary talents a sort of miniature D-8 Caterpillar tractor that he constructed from junk found on our homestead.

First he made an arc welder from an old aircraft engine and generator. Next he cut out and shaped 1,750 steel tracks for the treads, then mounted bogey wheels and hydraulic steering on an old two-wheel garden tractor. Parts he could not obtain he would pour in a sand mold and finish off with a file. To get Mike to defy the impossible, all one had to do was tell him he couldn't possibly do it. One accomplishment was his construction of a working model of what he called a Flopogyro. This device simulated a bird's beating wings and actually flew. Had it not beaten itself into kindling when landing somewhat askew, Mike had intended to construct a full-size working model. Few who knew him would wager he couldn't accomplish what Leonardo and legions of others could not.

Mike, like a magpie, scrounged and hoarded a store of disparate parts and pieces from which he seemingly could locate not only the kitchen sink but the entire kitchen. This became apparent after I flew a Grumman Widgeon with a load of cement to our homestead. Upon landing on the lake I encountered a long, slow swell, and after touching down porpoised upward in what can be a difficult situation in an amphibian. Fortunately, I stopped the porpoising after only one leap and taxied into the beach to unload. After toting a sack of cement to the cabin, I returned for another to be met by a startling sight. Most of the horizontal stabilizer was gone. The rooster tail of water kicked up by porpoising had sheared it off. I had to taxi the nine miles to Port Alsworth. There, to my amazement, Mike rummaged through his bone pile and extracted a complete Widgeon horizontal stabilizer, which he quickly installed and had me on my way.

In the 1960s Mike fled Babe's household to come serve as our caretaker at Miller Creek for a few years He did so, he contended, to escape daily harangues by Babe, who had late in life caught that virulent case of religion. At every meal Babe would implore the Good Lord with such intensity to enter Mike's sinful heart that the poor old fellow had trouble getting his food down. The latter dismaying circumstance prompted Mike to seek sanctuary at our place.

While here, at age sixty Mike married for the first time and took his sixty-nine-year-old bride, Viola, to live in a small guest cabin we had. Dominating the one ten-foot by twenty-foot room was Mike's first love, a huge metal lathe, which Viola blended into the decor by tastefully draping with a tablecloth when it was not in use. According to her, Mike was so enamored of her metal rival that he would have taken it into their bed if he had his way, along with the metal shavings she often had to pluck off the sheets.

It's a shame some wealthy "angel" did not turn Mike loose with unlimited funds. Had this happened, I've little doubt that long before anyone else, Mike would have split the atom, explored outer space, and perhaps invented the Internet. Despite Babe branding master-mechanic Mike unredeemable, I suspect Mike sneaked through the pearly gates, but only after first oiling its squeaking hinges, jimmying the locking device designed to bar sinners, and donning oversize celestial robes of sufficient length to obscure his feet of clay from the probing eyes of St. Peter.

ONE OLD LEGISLATIVE COLLEAGUE of mine had the unique and unenviable experience of suffering a massive heart attack in the 1970s while flying solo. Despite this diversion, Bill Poland was able to land safely at the Juneau airport.

Bill, who was from Kodiak, died in 1999 at the age of eighty-seven. Like myself, he had been a borough manager, state senator, pilot, and guide. He shared with me much bemusement and frustration with the sometimes ridiculous posturing accompanying much of the legislative process, which he likened to a stylized crane dance.

The airborne heart attack was not Bill's only unusual aircraft incident. One bright September day in the late '80s I was flying to one of my hunting camps on the Alaska Peninsula when I noted on the shores of lower Ugashik Lake what appeared to be an aircraft genuflecting toward the rising sun at the edge of the willows, its posterior pointed heavenward like a Muslim at prayer. Upon landing to investigate, however, the imprecations I heard were less likely excerpts from the Koran than from a Marine barracks. The "muezzin" proved to be Bill Poland.

"Can you imagine anyone overshooting ten miles of runway!" Bill fumed. "I feel like an idiot." He explained that he had spotted a fine bull moose at the edge of the lake and, realizing that his client would have difficulty making a stalk, decided to hold off landing as long as possible. Trouble was the sun was smack in his eyes and he didn't touch down until a bit late. They ended up in the same swamp the moose had discreetly vacated.

Back then, it was still legal to hunt on the same day you were airborne. And when Bill introduced me to his client, I understood why he'd elected to fly in as close to their quarry as possible. The client was an Austrian haus frau of monumental proportions. Her three hundred-plus pounds threatened at any moment to burst forth from the strained seams of her Loden green Tyrolean hunting garb, an eventuality that filled me more with dread than delight.

Bill's camp at Ugashik Narrows was but a short hop away and I offered to fly them there. Since my aircraft's back seats could not accommodate Brunhilde's bulk, we removed them. It took the combined efforts of me and Bill to boost her aboard the plane. Each of us grasped a gargantuan thew and with much grunting and groaning propelled her into the cockpit, where she sprawled unceremoniously, gasping for breath, then trussed her on the floor using some line to extend the pitifully inadequate reach of the seat belts. This was to be, I believe, Bill's last guided hunt. Shortly thereafter he suffered the heart attack, perhaps in belated response to the coronary abuse occasioned by the incident at Ugashik. At least in my own case, power-lifting that Teutonic titan brought on a case of lumbago that lasted a month!

6 People I seem to be

No longer in opposite corners, Wally Hickel
and I are now close friends. 1999

SOME OF THE MOST unforgettable people I've ever met apparently look like me. At least that's what some folks think. People often recognize my face, but they don't always know which name to put with it. During the *Exxon Valdez* trial for the 1989 spillage of oil in Alaska's Prince William Sound, an elderly gentleman came up to me, thrust out his hand, and said compassionately: "Good luck, Captain Hazelwood." Not wishing to disabuse him of his kindly gesture toward defendant Joseph Hazelwood, I simply thanked him and continued on.

The following winter, soon after Alaska icon Norman Vaughn returned from climbing a mountain in Antarctica named in his honor, a fellow came up to me and asked: "Hey Norm, when you going back to dig up those airplanes in Greenland?" He was referring to another of the indefatigable colonel's efforts, which was to retrieve some World War II aircraft deeply encapsulated within a Greenland ice field.

At least a dozen times I've been mistaken for my good friend Norman, who first made a name for himself by accompanying Admiral Richard Byrd to the South Pole in 1927. For this mistake I am flattered. Few folks have lived life so abundantly and in the process inspired the aging to recognize that decrepitude lies more in the mind than in the body. Would that I were more like him, an aspiration reflected in my response to a couple of women who came up to me in a restaurant and inquired: "Aren't you Norman Vaughn?"

"No, not yet, though I'm working at it," was my reply. "But do I really look like I'm over ninety?" Of course, Norman doesn't look over ninety either. His indulgent wife, Carolyn, says she's married to a perennial teenager. At this writing he's still driving dogs, cars, and snowmobiles with hair-raising abandon and looking forward to his first sip of champagne atop Mount Vaughn, which he hopes to summit again on his hundredth birthday, on December 19, 2006. I wouldn't bet against him making it.

Norman's zest for adventure was still apparent when at age ninety-two he was scheduled for heart surgery. He viewed it as just another exhilarating challenge. I recently visited Norman's booth at the Palmer State Fair, where he was signing books. A visitor to the booth asked, "Are you two teamed up?" "No," I responded, "but if we were, we ought to be over there," and I pointed to a tent bearing the sign "Alaska Fossils."

Not long ago a young fellow came up and gushed: "Governor, I've always wanted to shake your hand and thank you for all the wonderful things you've done for the state. Let me tell you, I think you're the finest governor we've ever had." Both flattered and embarrassed by his accolades, I was attempting to accept them with an appropriate show of humility when he administered the coup de grace to my ego. Having exhausted his paeans of praise, he again thrust out his hand and enthused: "Gee, it's been really great to meet you, Wally." Wally? Talk about one's balloon being rudely deflated. He'd confused me with ex-governor Wally Hickel!

But perhaps the ultimate in scrambling identities was reported by Norman Vaughn's wife, Carolyn. Someone had accosted Norman and asked: "Aren't you Jay Hickel?"

Actually, such confusion can prove a blessing since it serves to blur indiscretions that might otherwise prove embarrassing. For example, while a committee on which I served was awaiting our flight's arrival at the Juneau airport, member Charley Cole said: "Come on into the bar and I'll buy you guys a glass of wine." Barely avoiding being trampled in the ensuing rush, I hobbled in after the others on wobbly legs that I had long ago injured. Though I had nothing but a glass of tomato juice (Scout's honor), some twenty minutes later when I got up to leave I was staggering about like a drunken sailor, a sorry spectacle with which no self-respecting ex-Marine would ever wish to be identified. As I lurched out of the bar I swear I saw half the folks I knew in Juneau pass in review, smiling indulgently, no doubt thinking: "Ah, now we know! The *real* Hammond has finally surfaced."

Sure enough, a month or so later I was told that someone had asked: "Is Hammond now on the sauce? We saw him barely able to totter out of the airport bar." But with all the mistaken identities floating around, I can now tell people: "If you think you saw Hammond staggering out of a bar, you're certainly mistaken. It's bound to be either Joe, Norman, or Wally!"

I'LL CONFESS to at least two cases where my own ability to connect face and name became seriously compromised. During one of my political campaigns, a fellow came up, stuck out his hand, and said: "Hi, Jay. How are you?" Noting my blank look, he chided: "You don't remember my name, now do you?"

"The heck I don't," I told him, "I just can't place your face."

Even worse was an incident involving an old colleague of mine from the Fish and Wildlife Service, a fellow I'd not seen in years. At a book signing in Anchorage, I looked up from the table piled with copies of my autobiography to see him standing in line, awaiting his turn to meet the author. Knowing I could not confess to forgetting his name without crushing embarrassment, I frantically scrolled through my fading mental Rolodex, trying to come up with it. Bingo! Cal! Cal Lensink! My grateful relief prompted a shameless spate of "Cal this" and "Cal that" to evidence I'd not forgotten his name.

The next day I was at another signing when a person handed her copy of the book to me. "How would you like me to inscribe it?" I asked.

"Just sign it to . . . " And here she gave the name of the person who had been found guilty of murdering a friend of mine many years before. It was indeed the killer, a person I thought long ago dead, or at least still serving time. With my mind totally blown, I must have scribbled something, though I can't recall what. The few failing memory connections that remained to me promptly shortcircuited, a fact that became shockingly evident when I looked up to find my old Fish and Wildlife friend again standing in line. And I couldn't think of his name!

This time, that mental Rolodex refused to even materialize, much less flip open. How could I possibly confess I couldn't think of his name without seeming a blithering idiot, especially after having burbled it repeatedly the day before? Then I found a ray of hope: since I had signed four books for him yesterday, this one would probably be for some friend or relative.

"How would you like me to sign this one?" I asked, while enthusiastically welcoming him back.

"Just make it out to me," was his response. I was had!

IDENTITY PROBLEMS long predated my ascendance into some degree of public prominence. For many years I thought myself a shirttail relative of famed explorer Meriwether Lewis. This presumption was prompted by an inscription penciled in an old family Bible given my grandfather by his father, John Hammond. It read: "John Hammond, married to Marietta Lewis Hammond, daughter of Meriwether of Lewis and Clark fame."

Though aware that traveling too deeply among family tree roots might find some steeped in night soil, I've nonetheless plowed through every account, journal, and biography concerning old Meriwether. Somewhat to my dismay, I've found no evidence he ever married. Since marriage back then was far more a prerequisite for siring children than it is today, that alone calls the Bible inscription into question.

I conveyed this concern to my Aunt Edith, family historian and granddaughter of John, who had penciled that note in the Bible. She explained that shortly after the centennial celebration of the Lewis and Clark expedition, an old lady called upon her and her mother, Arabella Hammond, at their home in Albany, New York. The woman announced she had represented the Lewis clan at the centennial and, having there heard of Marietta Lewis Hammond's connection to Meriwether, decided to call on Hammond's daughter-in-law Arabella and Arabella's daughter, Edith, to tell them about it.

If we're truly related, Meriwether apparently dallied outside of wedlock. Hence I don't know what that makes me, but any status of illegitimacy I might have inherited has been filtered through four generations—no matter what my opponents might try to tell you. Far more discomfiting is the fact that if Meriwether Lewis and I are kin, destroyed is my contention that a penchant for politics is not a congenital defect lodged in Hammond genes. Though appointed, rather than elected, as governor of the Louisiana Purchase, Lewis was undeniably a politician, and one of somewhat less than noble dimensions. At one point he was summoned to Washington to explain some questionable handling of federal funds. En route somewhere on the remote Natchez Trace he was either murdered or, more likely, died by his own hand.

While my detractors have never suggested I do similar penance, I was once told I deserved a posthumous commendation, "and the sooner the better!"

DURING MY YEARS in public office I sometimes received letters from folks with the same hind name. From one I learned a vociferous critic might actually be a distant relative. My correspondent had enclosed a treatise titled "A Genealogy from the Town of Barton, Vermont." Cited therein were the meanderings of antecedent Elizabeth Penn Hammond, cousin of William Penn. Upon the death of her husband in 1632, young Elizabeth set sail from London for the New World on the bark *Griffin*. Accompanying were her son and daughter. Ultimately they wound up in Barton, Vermont, where the daughter married one Ebenezer Atwood.

Upon learning of this unholy union, I could not wait for an appropriate opportunity to ruin the day of my old friendly foe, *Anchorage Times* editor Robert Atwood—so I chose a most *inappropriate* time. It came during a public function honoring King Olaf of Norway. Bob and I shared the podium in greeting His Majesty. During my stint at the mike, I announced: "After years of friendly dispute, Bob, you and I had best beware of whose blood we shed in the future since it could be our very own. I have in hand a genealogy from the town of Barton, Vermont." I went on to cite the particulars, ending with: "So I hereby publicly acknowledge that at long last I'm prepared to cry 'Uncle,' Bob, now that you may well *be* my Uncle Bob."

With that Atwood demanded to see the document. Then, shaking his head in consternation, he confessed it *was* possible the noble Atwood bloodline might have been so sullied, since his antecedents had also come from that part of New England.

7 Floundering amid fins, feathers, & fur

Todd Sheldon holds up his twenty-six pound pike that
we ate on for a week.
Miller Creek, 1995; Bill Sheldon photo

WHEN I FIRST MET Larry Nicholson, I could whip him at almost anything, be it arm wrestling, horseshoes, weight lifting, or busting birds with a shotgun. Of course Larry was only fourteen at the time. Meanwhile, he's evolved from friend to one of the few I'd be proud to call son were it not for the humiliation he delights in heaping on me. So instead I wish he was the kid brother I never had so I could put him in his place on occasion.

Those occasions now are too few and far between. One such took place some years back while we were hunting waterfowl. I and the client I was guiding had our limit of geese while Larry had not one. After lunch the client and I headed to some duck ponds while Larry grimly strode off after geese. It wasn't long before we heard *blam!*, then *blam! blam! blam!* To our surprise, however, no birds flew up from where Larry was shooting.

Only later did a red-faced Larry 'fess up to shamefully unsportsmanlike behavior spurred by his determination not to go home empty-handed. Upon learning the truth, I thought it only proper to retrieve the trophy he'd neglected to claim and present it to him at his next birthday party, along with the following bit of verse:

Now some in their haste would commit wanton waste
And not salvage the game that they bag.
Or could it simply be that extreme modesty
Makes you reluctant to brag?

At any rate, here's a trophy of yours
The only one of its kind on the loose.
So take a grand bow while explaining just how
To ground-sluice an inanimate goose.

Along with that, in front of family and friends I handed him a well-peppered goose decoy. His humiliation was exquisite.

LARRY NICHOLSON shared with me the most hazardous sheep hunt I've ever guided, and thanks to him I survived to tell the tale. Larry had just returned from Vietnam, where he served in the Air Force's super-elite one-hundred-member pararescue combat team. Of the eight hundred applicants for training in Larry's class, he was one of only eight who successfully completed the arduous training. As a result Larry had acquired certain skills far exceeding mine; otherwise what I had intended to be my final sheep hunt could have as well been yet another stupid way to die.

There we were within a thousand feet of camp. Trouble was, that thousand feet was almost vertical. Trapped partway down a steep rock wall we could neither descend nor scale, night and thick snow were falling. As we clung precariously to a small outcropping, I cursed myself for gambling at stakes that could prove terminal.

That morning Larry and I, along with my client, Dr. Dee Heetderks of Bozeman, Montana, had bucked our way through heavy brush high into the sheep hills, only to have fog and wet snow move in to obscure our quarry. As it grew late, we noticed a stream that dropped sharply to our camp back at a lake. We chose to head down the stream rather than fight the witch-fingered alders that had clutched at us coming up. Although the stream fell steeply, we found the going fairly easy. At times the twisting route hid our destination, but as we rounded corner after corner, camp got ever closer.

With but one more obscuring twist to go, I debated sliding down a twenty-foot rock slab we encountered. What if around the next corner we could go no farther? To climb back up the slab appeared impossible. I didn't like the odds. "Sorry, we'd best go back the way we came. But it's too dark to travel now. We'll have to hole up here. Larry, get out the Visqueen. It'll at least keep us dry and fairly warm."

"The Visqueen? I thought *you* had it!"

Suddenly what seemed but another rough adventure assumed ominous dimensions. Though I wore a rain suit, neither Doc nor Larry had one. Both were soaking wet. Under plastic they could stave off hypothermia, but without it, they were in trouble. We were above timberline, so we had nothing to use in building a fire. There was no choice but to gamble with that twenty-foot wall, so we slid down it to the rocks below.

Rounding the next corner, my worst fears slugged us between the eyes. The stream plunged straight down another wall we could not possibly descend. Trapped on a ledge that seemed no bigger than a desktop, we could go neither up nor down. Now in the darkness, the snow falling, Doc and Larry clung to each other, with me on top trying to provide a weather shield. During the longest night I've ever spent we took turns exercising— very carefully. One time Doc slipped, and had we not grabbed him, he would have plunged to boulders a hundred feet below.

At dawn we crawled back to reassess the sheer rock face above us. No way could I or Doc get up it. Years younger and extremely strong, Larry said he'd try. Standing on my shoulders, he could just reach a small crevice. To our amazement, he chinned himself by what seemed a single finger to reach another hold. Incredibly he made it to the top. With several feet of nylon twine I used for packboard lashing, Larry made a bridle that appeared to my apprehensive eye as gossamer as a spiderweb. With that he hauled us up to his perch. Then we beat our way back down the way we had originally come, happily shaking hands with alders most of the way.

When I think back on the many people with whom I've shared the Alaska wilderness, I'll always remember one client of more than thirty years who evolved into such a good friend I was reluctant to charge him for my guide services. Somehow I managed to overcome that reluctance, despite the fact his mere presence and friendship were more than ample reward.

Todd Sheldon, owner of the famed Mepps spin-fishing lure company, was an indefatigable angler who came to Alaska each year. Though suffering from chronic arthritis, almost every fall Todd would spend a couple of weeks with us, field testing his products as well some new joint in his body in the wake of eleven major operations. Both shoulders, elbows, and knees had been replaced. Other appendages received lesser overhauls. He once suggested that doctors should simply discard *all* his old original parts and wire up new ones, just so long as he could still stuff them into a pair of chest waders.

Todd and I shared many adventures and misadventures, such as the time when crawling through heavy brush that I accidentally knelt on some alders that were obscuring a sleeping brown bear. The creature, provoked by having his nap disturbed, propelled me into Todd, who was crawling a few feet from my rear with his movie camera. His comment: "I know I asked you to get me close enough to a bear to get some good shots, but I wanted to take them from *outside* the bear looking in, not vice versa."

Each year Todd kept coming back, despite being subjected to this and numerous other indignities. I suspect the only reason he tolerated the abuse I inflicted on him was to stay close to Bella's cooking. On a strict diet, Todd said he prepared for his time with us by virtually starving himself for a month so that with some degree of good conscience he could indulge freely. And that he did. Every day Bella would bake him his favorite, rhubarb pie. Her bread was another attraction. At breakfast, slice after slice of toast slathered with moss berry jelly and peanut butter would slowly inflate both Todd's waders and beneficent smile until his boys, Bill and Mike, would remind him they were up there to fish, and virtually drag him kicking from the table.

Todd himself was a fine cook and taught us a thing or two. One day, for example, he said if he could get a pike of twenty-five pounds or more he'd like to have it mounted to add to his collection of Alaska trophies. "What's more," he told us, "I'll make fish chowder for you out of that pike." Neither Bella nor I were enthralled. I had eaten pike years before back east and thought them too bony and fishy for my taste.

When Todd caught a twenty-six pounder, he made good on his threat. After skinning the fish and salting its hide, I watched him fillet it. This he did expertly, leaving it totally boneless. He also removed skin and fat. The chowder was superb and prompted Bella and me to have three bowls each. We ate on that huge pike for several days, first as chowder, then broiled or baked. It was as good a fish as we had ever tasted, far better than salmon or trout. Most others who have learned how to prepare pike properly reach the same conclusion.

During one fall at election time, Todd, his son Bill, and I were forced by bad weather to land at the little village of Levelock. While awaiting for the fog to clear, we were accosted by an obviously inebriated young lady who wanted us to "party." I assured her that were it not for the fact I was flying, I would be delighted to accommodate so beguiling a creature. My remarks fell flat, and with a scathing look and toss of her head, she screeched: "I no vote for you, Jay Hammond!"

Todd found all this immensely entertaining, and henceforth whenever I goofed or did something that especially caught his attention, he would repeat the young lady's threat. Should I be so fortunate as to gain access to paradise, where fine trout streams must surely abound, I suspect I'll have no trouble locating Todd. All I'll have to do is pack with me a rhubarb pie, waft it about, and listen for someone to loudly chortle: "I no vote for you, Jay Hammond!"

8Survivor

A couple of hours as a guest in an Air Force F-15 made this old
WW II pilot feel as anachronistic as a frontier Indian fighter.
Elmendorf Air Force Base, Anchorage, 1980; U.S. Air Force photo

AS MIGHT BE EXPECTED of a man with more than half a century of jockeying aircraft, some of my closest encounters occurred while saddled in a cockpit. The most recent entailed the pretzeling of my old Cessna 180 in the summer of 2000. I was returning from Anchorage to our Lake Clark homestead with a load of supplies after a long stay in town recuperating from hip surgery. The weather was beautiful and the light wind blew right down our airstrip. The Good Book says pride goeth before a fall, and I proved it.

As I gently touched down, I congratulated myself on such a slick landing, since I had not flown in the past several weeks. "Not bad for an old gaffer," I thought smugly. But *smug* turned to *ugh* when, after the plane rolled about thirty feet, the left gear leg snapped. The Cessna performed a violent vertical ground loop and ploughed upside down for another fifty feet to an undignified shuddering halt. It was my shortest landing since I flew off aircraft carriers during World War II.

Suspended upside down by my seat belt and shoulder straps, I attempted to unsnap them in order to reach the ignition switch and turn it off to avoid fire. After what seemed like half an hour, I was finally able to undo my belt and drop on my head to the aircraft's upside-down ceiling. Both doors were jammed, and dribbling gas starting to baste my head and shoulders. With an aversion to ending up a "crispy critter" as added inducement, I was able to kick a door free and crawl out.

In trying to figure out what had gone wrong, I first thought a wheel had come off in flight, since it was nowhere to be seen. However, later it was found some two hundred feet away in a swale alongside the runway. I then learned that it wasn't uncommon for a gear leg to break at the top two bolts holding the axle. Apparently old Cessna gear—particularly when used with ski-wheels in rough places, as mine had been for years—sometimes crystallizes and snaps at that particular point. Some had snapped while the planes were just taxiing. Thus I wished that the ensuing newspaper account had not been headlined "Governor Flips Aircraft," but rather had stated the more accurate "Aircraft Flips Governor."

The only happy aspect of this sorry experience was that my insurance agent had talked me into boosting my coverage by several thousand dollars just a few months before and I had not yet replaced my old engine with a new one nor painted the aircraft as I had considered. That latter intent was prompted by assertions of my querulous good friend Ed Painter that my plane had the ugliest paint job in Alaska: "urine yellow, corpse white, and bile black." Upon learning of my unorthodox landing that totaled the aircraft, Ed commented: "Jeez, what some guys will do to avoid a new paint job."

A fellow ex-Marine and state game warden, Ed helps keep me humble. He relishes pointing out what I fear is too often true: "You know, in my business I've learned there are four breeds of bandits you can't trust at all:

guides, commercial fishermen, politicians, and attorneys. And Hammond is three out of four. 'Nuff said."

In retaliation, at his retirement dinner, after introducing Ed as the youngest cantankerous old man I've ever known, I was both dismayed and delighted to inadvertently dump a pitcher of iced tea in his lap.

I SPEAK FROM VAST EXPERIENCE when I say that nothing grabs your attention more than the failure of an aircraft engine in flight. Upon the occasion of my thirteenth, a reporter asked me to catalog such mishaps. It was surprisingly easy to remember them all. Only the first engine failure resulted in damage to the aircraft. That was in 1946 when the engine on my 1929 vintage Loening amphibian disemboweled itself just over the trees on Shirley Lake near Rainy Pass and compelled me to steer between two spruce trees, shucking wings en route. Mute testimony of this event resides in a hangar at the Alaska Aircraft Museum on Lake Hood, where the craft was hauled by helicopter some twenty years after the event.

My fourteenth engine failure was almost catastrophic. It occurred one windy morning in 1992 when I had to fuel my floatplane at our Lake Clark dock, on which I had stashed two five-gallon cans of gas, where they had sat exposed to rainy weather for several weeks. Normally I fuel up in Anchorage or Port Alsworth rather than wrestle gas cans up onto the wing to strain fuel through an old chamois-lined funnel to filter out water. Having acquired a new state-of-the-art funnel recommended to replace chamois, I used it for the first time. After dumping in the contents of both cans, I noted an inch of water lodged in the funnel. After rocking the wings of the Cessna 180, I drained all three of its fuel sumps to see if other water had filtered through. Nothing but pure gasoline flowed from their ports.

Heavy wave action prevented takeoff from the main lake, so I taxied from our sheltered bay around the corner to the lee of some islands. Climbing to about five hundred feet into a thirty-knot easterly wind, I turned 180 degrees to the west. Almost immediately after I reached the point from which I could no longer return to land in the islands' lee, my engine conked out. A screaming silence descended in which I could hear only teeth chattering.

With nowhere to land but in trees or rough waves, I frantically checked my fuel tank selector, pumped the primer, and hit the starter button. The engine restarted reluctantly, but only by goosing the primer and throttle was I able to keep from going into the trees. This technique worked for only a minute or two, however, and I was forced to decide whether to opt for a treetop landing or take my chances in the rough water. It appeared I could just make it to a point where I could land next to a beach quartering to the wind, where the surf was less violent. I set down on the rough water. The plane bounced repeatedly, then ceased bucking. After securing a line to the wing strut, I leaped into water up to my neck, and made my way to the beach, and hauled the reluctant aircraft to shore.

Once again checking my fuel quick-drains, I was dumbfounded when water poured out. Only after draining at least two quarts did a steady stream of gas flow. I was then able to start the engine and allow it to run for a few minutes before I again shut it down, rocked the wings, and recommenced draining water. I went through this cycle four times before I ceased getting water. Then I radioed the folks at Port Alsworth and told them I was going to try to fly across the lake to their community. "If you don't hear from me in an hour, perhaps you could take a look?"

On takeoff I bounced into the air and clawed for altitude prior to crossing the mile of turbulent water between myself and Port Alsworth. At two thousand feet the engine quit again, but I was able to make it into the sheltered waters of Port Alsworth's Hardenberg Bay. After drifting backward onto the beach, I again checked my fuel drains—and found more water. I repeated wing-rocking, draining the sumps and briefly running the engine. Only after several such procedures did I again hazard a takeoff. While the engine did not quit again during the ensuing several days, each time I checked the fuel drains I got water. For some time thereafter, my route of flight resembled that of a besotted bumblebee bouncing from flower to flower as I wove from lake to lake—just in case.

Later in checking my new plastic funnel, I found that water streamed through its alleged filter. Feeling obligated to warn other pilots, I wrote an article, published by the *Anchorage Daily News,* in which I told about my fourteen engine failures and the role played by the funnel in the latest debacle. This elicited an indignant letter to the editor from a fellow who was huckstering this product. "It's not the funnel that is the hazard," he fumed. "It's Hammond. Fourteen engine failures? My God! He's virtually *raining* aircraft out of the sky on an unsuspecting public. If he simply had read the instructions embossed on the funnel he'd know the product is not authorized for aircraft fuel."

Sure enough, after the fine print extolling the funnel's filtration features and warning against using it to strain mixed outboard-motor gas since the oil therein would nullify its water filtration capability, it indeed said: "Not authorized for aircraft fuel." This seemed rather peculiar, since aircraft product suppliers were marketing it. What in the world, I wondered, was it designed to filter out if not water? Perhaps coffee grounds and spruce needles?

CHUCK DICOSTANZA, who ran the U.S. Fish and Wildlife research program for Bristol Bay in the years just before Alaska statehood, was my unwilling accomplice in a memorable aircraft close call in 1957.

Chuck had received reports of someone breaking into one of his field camps at Ugashik Lake, and I flew him down to inspect the damage. The following account of the ensuing fiasco is a shorter version of the article I wrote for Fred Hirschman's splendid book *Bush Pilots of Alaska.*

The snow cover on Ugashik Lake stretched unblemished for miles, save for a single set of ski tracks near the shore. The thermometer taped to the wing strut read minus 22 Fahrenheit. I circled twice to check the tracks for overflow. If water was present, the tracks would be darker than the surrounding snow. Spotting no sign of this hazardous condition, I prepared to land.

There was no wind, and we settled into old ski tracks and taxied toward the beach. Suddenly, with a gut-wrenching crunch, our right ski dropped through the ice, tilting the Piper PA14 up on one wing. "You better get out!" I shouted unnecessarily to Chuck, who was already struggling with the single door to his right. Forgetting to first unhook his seat belt, he floundered futilely for a moment.

A second crunch and the left ski went through the ice. We were sitting up to our puckered navels in searing cold water. Chuck finally flipped loose his seat belt and dove out the door, rudely propelled by my right foot. Ice cakes blocked his way, but he plunged beneath and came up in front of the right wing. I came up behind it gasping like a beached whale.

Our winter flight suits of down immediately began to encase us in armor plate as they froze. Climbing atop the wings, which now sprawled flat on the ice, we crawled out on the left wing and gingerly tested the ice. As we walked toward shore, the ice sagged at every step, but it held. There was a cabin two hundred yards away, and we lumbered toward it, hair frozen into helmets and extremities bone-white with cold.

We opened the unlocked door with brittle fingers and checked the small oil stove. No oil. A search revealed no matches either. I cracked out of my flight pants and fumbled into an inner pocket with the gray sticks that were my fingers. I forked out my waterproof match case and somehow got it open. Shredding some old magazines, we fired them up in the stove's oil pot and fed in twigs of alder, a wood that burns fairly well green. Pain scorched to the surface as we began to thaw. We slumped naked on gas crates, then started to laugh like idiots, surprised we were still alive.

For two nights and days we fed the fire but remained unfed ourselves. The cabin had no food, and though caribou roamed within gunshot, we had no means of killing one. Chuck, an avid smoker, found a can of stale coffee, rolled some in a *Playboy* magazine centerfold, and lit it, almost asphyxiating both of us.

On our first day at the cabin, patches of ice fog rolled in. We heard an aircraft high overhead but couldn't see it, and ice conditions kept the plane from landing to investigate. Later we learned that my wife, Bella, had received a report that our wrecked plane had been sighted but that there was no sign of survivors. Next morning, however, the sky was clear. A search aircraft landed nearby to pick us up, and we were flown to Naknek.

I can't say the same for the airplane, which later dropped through the ice into twelve feet of water. When I was finally able to return several months later for a full salvage attempt, we found the plane on the beach, trashed by rubble ice that had rolled it ashore. I was able to salvage only the plane's skis, propeller, and engine.

GOING THROUGH THE ICE at Ugashik Lake was but one of several times when I thought I might drown. One of the most harrowing occurred in storm-tossed waters off Kodiak Island. At the time I was doing a television show called *Jay Hammond's Alaska,* and the show's crew and I had flown to the village of Ouzinkie during Russian Christmas to interview and film the revered Orthodox priest Father Peter Kreta. A storm prevented us from flying back to the town of Kodiak, so Father Peter radioed a Kodiak-bound crab boat and asked them to divert to Ouzinkie and pick us up.

At the height of the storm and in deep darkness, the crabber arrived. The small rust bucket looked to me to be far from adequate for handling some of the world's most dangerous fishing grounds. My concern increased exponentially when a villager announced: "Oh, we know that boat. It's a soaker."

"What do you mean, a soaker?" I asked.

"It capsized last year. But it now has stabilizers so it should be OK."

With some trepidation, I and my crew, along with the Kreta family and several villagers, climbed aboard and crowded the tiny cabin. Once out of Ouzinkie's harbor we felt the full brunt of the storm. When someone lit up a cigarette, several passengers already struggling with sea sickness fled the cabin to join me on the rear deck.

Increasingly mountainous waves crashed into the small vessel like monstrous black sea-horse stallions plunging at the quivering flanks of a terrified filly. As we bucked toward Kodiak, I clung to a stanchion to keep on my feet, fervently praying the new stabilizers would keep the boat from capsizing. Suddenly over the storm's banshee howl came a shuddering *whump!* Out of the cabin burst a wall-eyed deck hand, shouting: "My God! We hit a rock and we're short on survival suits!"

Instantly all poetic equine musings stampeded, to be replaced by the sobering realization that, as the oldest person aboard, I might be deemed by the others to be the most expendable. Emulating those gallant men on the *Titanic* who stepped aside for women and children was one thing, but I was unsure I could with grace defer to other adult males. Besides, times had changed and the only politically correct discrimination allowed was supposed to be on *behalf* of us elders. And what about the old seafaring tradition where the captain goes down with the ship? Strapping hulk that he was, it seemed unlikely I could talk, much less shuck him out of, his survival suit nor did I want those who might survive to report that their last view of Hammond was of him battling some frail old Aleut grandmother over possesion of hers. So what to do?

Fortunately, the distraught crewman returned and shrieked the good news: "It wasn't a rock after all; just the anchor broke loose and was thumping!"

Bless you, Father Peter, for being aboard. I suspect your celestial imprecations did more to assure safe passage to Kodiak than did the combined prayers of all of us other sinners.

WHAT COULD WELL HAVE BEEN the final close encounter occurred one fall evening in 1998 when I was flying home through Lake Clark Pass. Traffic through this gateway to the popular hunting and fishing grounds of Bristol Bay had increased enormously with the establishment of many lodges in southwestern Alaska. Accordingly, most pilots are especially alert going through the narrow confines of the pass. It's common practice to leave one's landing lights on and advise other pilots of your presence by radio, and aircraft rights of way are rigidly observed.

On this particular evening I was properly skirting the right side of the pass, all lights on and doubly alert since the sun was shining directly into my eyes. Just past the narrows I spotted two aircraft on the opposite side of the pass, heading eastward a comfortable distance to my left. As I turned to once again squint straight ahead, a Piper Super Cub roared over the top of me, its huge wheels seemingly no more than five feet from my windshield. I had the right of way, but that would have been little solace had the two planes embraced, thought I as I shuddered the rest of the way home, wondering how badly I might have soiled my britches.

9 Odd encounters

Challenging my narrow 1978 primary victory, the arguments of
Edgar Paul Boyko fall on deaf ears before the Alaska Supreme Court.
Juneau, 1978; Sally Sudduck photo

A COUPLE OF THE MOST BIZARRE encounters of my life involved, indirectly, an erstwhile political opponent of mine, attorney Edgar Paul Boyko. Though folks are wondrously generous, forgiving, or forgetful now that I am out of political office, there are some who will happily unsheathe ground axes with little provocation. Perhaps the most adroit at wielding same is Boyko, Wally Hickel's first attorney general, who took great exception to my having referred to him in *Tales of Alaska's Bush Rat Governor* as "near brilliant."

"That's the same as calling me stupid," Boyko groused to our mutual friend, the acerbic talk-show host Herb Shainlin.

Accolades can become a bit cloying, if not self-deluding, but I have been spared these by Boyko, who can always be counted on to expose my imperfections. His letter to the editor of an Anchorage paper in response to a laudatory article about me is but one example. It went something like this:

"Hammond's no hero of mine! He's a blatant political opportunist who, among other misdeeds, stole the election from Wally Hickel in 1978." He went on with considerable passion to accuse me of numerous sins of omission and commission orchestrated with Machiavellian connivance to embellish my public image at the expense of the public weal. Like an accomplished trial lawyer (which he was) interrogating a hostile witness, Boyko stripped my image of any possible redeeming virtue.

Once, in the wake of a diatribe on Boyko's weekly radio talk show, self-labeled *Roar of the Snow Tiger,* an elderly woman came up to me and asked: "Who's this man Bilko and why is he saying all those bad things about you?" Henceforth I always referred to Ed as Sergeant and to his program as *Spoor of the Snow Tiger.*

Our relationship was not improved when I spotted him in the front row at an Anchorage Chamber of Commerce luncheon I was addressing and took the occasion to tell about a startling experience I had in Tokyo in which he might, conceivably, have been involved. While attending a fishery conference, I was walking with biologists Steve Pennoyer and Ed Heiser, plus Ed's wife Marge, from our hotel past the compound of the Japanese premier. Heiser asked one of several attending policemen if it would be all right to take pictures. Granted permission, Ed set up his camera and commenced shooting from the sidewalk fronting the compound.

Suddenly we heard a strident scream, and from around the corner of the stone wall hurtled a wild-eyed apparition. Clutched in its right fist was a bomb the size of a shot put from which dangled a spluttering fuse! Virtually caroming off my shoulder, the bomb thrower raced through the gate and, along with incomprehensible shrieked imprecations, hurled his bomb at the premier's residence. Steve, Marge, and Ed hit the deck to join me in the gutter where I'd been dumped by the assailant's impact.

At once four Japanese policemen attached themselves like limpets to the bomber's frantically flailing appendages. For a moment I feared we were about to witness a drawing and quartering. Instead they tossed the man into a metal cage while a fifth policeman scurried toward the bomb, holding a protective shield before him. While he was yet a few feet away, the bomb exploded with a dyspeptic, harmless *pop*, spewing forth a billow of crimson smoke.

Immediately thereafter the gates were slammed shut, leaving us to wonder what in the world was going on? Next day we were enlightened. The *Tokyo Times* noted that the man in custody was a renegade member of a right-wing extremist organization known as—this is true—the Boykoists, a group that advocates independence for Okinawa.

"So now, Ed," I said to Boyko in front of the laughing Chamber of Commerce members, "I finally know just what you've been up to of late, and I welcome your attention being diverted from me to a far greater cause."

Boyko and I were not always at odds. Some years prior to my having alienated him by "stealing" the 1978 gubernatorial election, Boyko had elicited my aid in the defrocking of a dentist who was discovered to have had five patients die through the administration of anesthetics in the absence of a qualified anesthesiologist. One case was especially bizarre. Allegedly one Christmas Eve a man brought his wife to the dental office for some relatively minor emergency treatment. He remained in his car to keep the engine running in the bitter cold while his wife went inside. Finally the man went in to check on her. After fifteen minutes or so in the waiting room, the dentist was said to have breezed by and in passing remark rather casually: " Oh, by the way, I'm sorry to say we lost your wife."

This death prompted an investigation that revealed four other patients had succumbed in the dentist's chair. Unaware of such circumstances, I had been a patient of this bungler! Boyko, who was representing plaintiffs in a lawsuit against the doctor, requested a statement regarding my experience. In my case, x-rays had revealed four impacted wisdom teeth at ninety degrees to other molars. On the film, the teeth looked for all the world like toppled gravestones abutting a row of markers in a cemetery. Excavation rather than erection was required, according to the doctor.

I thought it a bit unusual that the doctor did not even inquire if I'd had any experience with the sodium pentathol he intended to use. I thought it more unusual still that he alone would, in essence, administer the anesthetic with one hand while doing surgery with the other. Not even a nurse, much less an anesthesiologist, was in attendance. Some four hours later, when Bella and a friend came to pick me up, they were aghast. I looked like I'd gone a few fast rounds with Joe Louis (the ex-heavyweight champ who, believe it or not, I once hit and staggered—but that's another story.) My head was bloated, my jaw was numb for days; I had trouble coordinating my movements.

As in most of his courtroom efforts, Boyko was successful, and the dentist was defrocked and retired from practice post haste. This was about the only time Boyko and I read from the same sheet of music. Always marching to his own drumbeat, Ed later became head of the Alaska Independence Party when that position was vacated by the death of Joe Vogler. Ill health has now stifled the Snow Tiger's roar. That's a shame. Colorful, articulate voices like Boyko's are needed to prick pompous asses, espouse outrageous causes, and keep the complacent from starting to believe their own copy.

RATHER THAN LEAVING readers to scoff at the assertion I once rocked Joe Louis, let me explain. Shortly after Bella and I were married, we were in New York City visiting my parents, who were vacationing there. One morning, while returning to our hotel room, I was rubbernecking when I accidentally bumped into a man coming out of a restaurant foyer. My profuse apologies amplified when I saw that the man was heavyweight boxing champion Joe Louis. Rather than decking me on the spot, the Brown Bomber simply smiled and graciously shrugged it off, leaving me with yet another tale to embellish.

There's also the time that Bella and I went window-chopping. Having no car of our own, we had borrowed an old Plymouth with a push-button shift mechanism. "The starter doesn't always catch," the owner warned us. "When it doesn't, you have to go under the hood and jump across the terminals with a pair of pliers."

In making the rounds of several Anchorage stores, the starter gave us no trouble. However, as we tried to drive away from Blaine's paint store in Spenard, it chose to give up the ghost. Grabbing pliers, I pulled the hood latch and piled out. "Now, when I get the pliers in place, you turn the key on," I instructed Bella. "Just make sure the push button's in neutral or it won't start." Using the pliers to short out the starter I could get the engine to grind away, but it stubbornly refused to kick in.

"Have you got the key on? Is the push button in neutral?"

"Yes," was Bella's impatient reply on both counts.

"It must be flooded," I said. "Hold the gas pedal down and I'll give it another try."

With that I applied the pliers and the engine roared into life, powering the auto as it leaped the eight-inch curb and rocketed through Blaine's plate-glass front window, ending up in a cascade of glass amid a gaggle of horrified customers. Thankfully the beast stalled out before it did further violence and, hood agape and grinning, crouched there spewing steam.

Picking myself up from the gravel where I'd been roughly deposited, I avoided the inclination to flee and manfully stepped through the window to face the owner's ire and a dressing down from my wife. Instead, I found Bella shaken virtually wordless, and the owner so graciously sympathetic that one would have assumed our spectacular entry was a common occurrence.

PART TWO

Rocking the ship of state

Be forewarned, all ye who enter this section of the book; those seeking insight, uplift, or intellectual stimulation will find little sustenance. Instead you'll be forced to pick your way past spoor left in the wake of foraging legislative bodies long extinct. Hence, step carefully, and best stay upwind! Though many referenced legislators are gone, all played roles in molding Alaska and warrant at least a nod in passing. Believing they would prefer their memory trigger a smile rather than a tear, I ask that you consider this section more roast than requiem—stories told both in prose and poetry for a per verse Alaska history lesson. While the names may be unfamiliar today, there is enough generically ridiculous, sublime, or disturbing about politics to warrant inclusion of some of their antics. Besides, in the world of politics, things simply have not changed that much.

10 Stumbling aboard

Ready for more fun, the second Alaska State Legislature posed
in 1961. I'm in the middle row, second from right.

IN 1959, UNENCUMBERED by either political experience or wisdom, I brought little baggage with me to the floor of the House of the first Alaska state Legislature. What I did bring ill-equipped me to enter that arena and hope to emerge unscathed during my freshman year as a legislator.

At first I was surprised that reasoned debate and statesmanship did not always dominate. My idealistic presumption had been that most legislators placed the public interest paramount. And while that faith has been sorely tested, I still believe such is the intent of most legislators when first elected. Only later—as perception grows that they may not be reelected should they place public interests ahead of special interests—does the recognition come that often to be a "successful" politician, one must rise *above* principle on behalf of politics. Particularly adept at such levitation are some legislators who are attorneys by profession. Nor is that their only prestidigitative power. Their ability to translate black into white can rival the biblical conversion of water into wine.

Since it is considered cardinal sin among legislators to directly question a fellow legislator's veracity or impugn a colleague's motives, I sought means of doing so *indirectly*—and stumbled on the device of rude verse. Comment that would have drawn censure if stated outright often sneaked by in ridiculous rhyme. By the time my target felt penetration, the average thirty-second attention span of the other legislators had been exceeded, and any outraged retort fell flat.

For example, our first Speaker of the House, Warren Taylor, a Fairbanks Democrat, was a rabidly partisan attorney who often "re-Taylored" legislation to accommodate clients—apparently deeming such not a "conflict" but rather a "compatibility" of interest. Taylor, in carrying Governor Bill Egan's water, heatedly opposed my efforts to create a board of fish and game and a board of education and sometimes twisted the rules in the process. Also, as one of the oldest members in the Legislature, Taylor seemed to suffer, albeit selectively, from an affliction common to those of advanced years. I noted this in the wake of his response to a voice vote on an amendment I had proposed, when he ruled that my motion lost.

Amendment votes,
while made by voice,
Are often nice and clear;
Yet somehow do not register
The same on every ear!

Many of my fellow freshman legislators joined me in feeling confused and disenchanted by a process that often rewarded those least deserving while subordinating truth and justice to chicanery, monetary reward, or political expediency. To avoid further confusion I eventually offered them the following advice:

When convictions of conscience determine your vote,
Brother, you're simply not smart.

You better line up and join with the team,
For you might as well know from the start

That while we admire great character strength
Moral courage, absence of fear

Strong purpose, integrity, honor, and guts . . .
We just ain't got *time* for them here!

Having no party affiliation, I entered the Legislature as one of two Independents. The other was Harold Hansen, who was an irascible curmudgeon from the small fishing community of Cordova. Hansen's delight in verbally eviscerating those imprudent enough to question his motives or to pontificate on matters in which they felt themselves better versed earned him the nickname Horrible. Since pontification and the impugning of motives are traits common to most politicians, Horrible found ample fare for filleting.

At these times his commercial fishing experience served him well. Casting his net in rebuttal, he'd haul in a school of flopping, goggle-eyed colleagues who were then merrily beheaded and slimed before being released. Horrible took no prisoners. Despite this abuse, most members held Hanson in high regard and no little awe. Though almost daily marinated in ethanol, even half drunk he could walk a shorter and straighter line between two points than most of us.

With Horrible and I as the only two Independents among sixty legislators, it soon became apparent little heed would be paid our presence unless we aligned with one party or the other. Moreover, he and I were often on opposite sides philosophically. This awareness prompted the following:

I wish Horrible Hansen would vote as I do
At least on one issue this year.
Else voters find out, that lout cancels out lout
And then kick us *both* out of here!

Sometimes legislative action, or inaction, proved irresistibly provocative and I would request "privilege of the floor" to offer an observation—in verse. These almost always appeared in the newspaper the next day. This did little to enhance my image as a statesman. Frequently upon returning to my district I'd hear reports of disgruntled constituents complaining: "If Hammond would only spend as much time working for our roads, schools, etc. as he did writing that stupid poetry we'd sure be a lot farther ahead."

Not everyone criticized my poetry so directly. Others were so polite in their censure that until it sunk in, it felt almost like a compliment. *Anchorage Daily News* reporter Sheila Toomey, for instance, once wrote an article in which she observed that I exhibited an "endearing affinity for truly bad verse."

When Alaska's election code was altered to make it far more difficult to win as an Independent, Horrible Hansen joined the Democrats and I the Republicans. I gave up my independent status with reluctance. While trying to decide which party to join, I had reached the disquieting conclusion I could have joined either and still have voted precisely the same on almost all issues. Both parties embraced ultraliberals and extreme conservatives, as well as admixtures such as myself who deem themselves fiscal conservatives but are branded liberals for our views on conservation.

It is on this ground of conservation that I fail to find solid footing in the camp of those who term themselves political conservatives. At one time I naively felt that because of the common word root, a true conservative would, like Teddy Roosevelt, embrace conservation over uninhibited exploitation. Instead, most who deem themselves conservatives today scoff at concern over environmental issues like land and water abuse, global warming, endangered species, and population excess.

Certainly some of these matters are overblown by extremists who forget that environmental health must include not only the physical environs but also those of a social nature dealing with body, mind, and spirit. Nonetheless, when I joined the Republican Party I felt I suffered from a split stance: one foot in the Democrat camp when it came to environmental issues and one in the Republican when it came to fiscal matters. Such a precarious posture did little to incline either party to embrace me.

WILLIAM A. EGAN, a grocery store owner from Valdez, was Alaska's first elected governor, taking office in 1959. Avuncular, tireless, and passionate in his determination to advance what he thought best for the new state, Democrat Egan was the consummate politician. His ability to remember not only every constituent's name but also most of their family members was legendary, and sorely envied by other politicians.

The monumental task of constructing an entire state government from blueprints contained in Alaska's newly ratified constitution was facilitated by Egan having presided over the constitutional convention. Deemed a model document by many political scientists (particularly those who had helped construct it), it drew heavily on counsel provided by the Public Administration Service think tank. A primary theme of PAS was to focus maximum power and accountability in the governor's office. One means suggested was to abolish the multitude of boards and commissions that in other states had achieved a degree of autonomy that served to screen them from gubernatorial overview.

It was on this issue Egan and I first locked horns. I believed both the Departments of Education and of Fish and Game should be at least a half step removed from the political arena since, to be effective, each requires greater continuity of program and insulation from political manipulation than do other state agencies. Such cannot be achieved if a new commissioner is automatically appointed with every change of administration, and programs are abandoned before given time to work.

Virtually every professional educator and biologist shared this view. As one of the latter, I had too often been affronted by "ballot biologists" in elective office who placed politics paramount when it came to fish and game management. I recalled actions taken by Alaska's territorial Legislature, enacting bounties on wolves, coyotes, wolverines, Dolly Varden trout, seals, and even our national emblem, the bald eagle. While in the Territorial Legislature, Egan had earned the title Eagle Bill for having introduced a measure increasing the bounty on eagles—a fact that did little to persuade me he should have total power over fish and game management.

Alaska's constitution made ample provision to erect the political screen I felt required. The constitution permits a department to be headed either by an individual or a board. In either case, the head—whether an individual or a board—would be appointed by and serve at the governor's pleasure. When a board headed the department, it, not the governor, would select a commissioner, who then served at the board's pleasure.

In arguments with Egan I pointed out that even with a board, it was still possible for him to get rid of a commissioner that he didn't want. "Since the board serves at your pleasure, should you wish to can the commissioner, all you have to do is reconstitute the board with members who feel as you do."

Egan was aghast: "But that would be political suicide!"

"Precisely," I responded.

Neither Egan nor I won all the marbles on this issue. My proposal creating a board for education passed. My bill to do the same for fish and game was modified to grant a board the authority to promulgate regulations, while the department was headed by a commissioner selected by the governor from a list of names presented by the board. Board members could be dismissed by the governor, but only for cause; the commissioner could be fired by the governor at his whim.

Later I did further violence to the governor's anti-board philosophy by successfully introducing legislation that created a multitude of local fish and game advisory boards. I believe in the end even Egan agreed that without a board to shelter the governor from political onslaught by every self-described fish and game expert, he'd have little time for other matters. Certainly every subsequent governor attempting to override fish and game management directives has been parboiled for doing so.

11 A motley crew

In the legislature, Clem Tillion was both my strong right arm
and my left foot. The latter he'd happily apply to the
hindquarters of opponents at my slightest suggestion.
Juneau, 1964

DURING THE FORMATIVE YEARS for the state of Alaska, an array of colorful characters strode, sneaked, or slithered about the legislative decks. I remember them fondly, some more than others of course, in the mellowing twilight of my own sunset years. Among the more colorful was Bob Blodgett, a Democrat known as the Heller from Teller, the tiny village northeast of Nome where he owned a store. As a member of the finance committee, Blodgett was expert in extracting far more than his district's share from state coffers. When castigated for this by envious colleagues, he would deliver rebuttal laced with malapropisms and scorn.

One of Blodgett's most noteworthy acts was his vow to fast until legislation establishing a school hot lunch program was released from committee and brought to a vote. The prospect of Blodgett withering away while his bill languished in committee had much appeal. However, despite the inclination of many lawmakers to bury the measure more deeply, it was finally exhumed and passed.

Sen. John Rader was one of the few legislators viewed by most as a statesman. I shared this view of the Anchorage Democrat, despite the fact I usually lost in floor debate with him. So sincere and intelligent seemed most of his arguments that I often threw in my hand and let him steal the pot, even though I held a full house to his pair of deuces. So persuasive was Rader, he once beguiled Republicans to support, and thereby glean undue blame for, an unpopular tax measure that at the last minute he opposed.

John Rader invited us all to sit
Bravely 'longside him and ride a bit
On a bandwagon which in reality hath
Been headed, I fear, down a primrose path.

For when it comes down to the wire we finally see
Foxy Johnny himself has decided to flee
And we suddenly find we're alone, with a start,
Not on a bandwagon at all, but a manure cart.

Among the legion of lawyers in the Legislature, John S. Hellenthal was perhaps our most artfully articulate philosophical prostitute. This Democrat from Anchorage could argue opposing positions on any issue with equal passion and persuasion. While his barrister brethren might occasionally make wine of water, John could convert garbage to gold, and vice versa.

A prime supporter of the idea to eliminate boards and commissions, he and I frequently clashed. Initially his courtroom tactics overwhelmed this country boy; however, when it became apparent Hellenthal was sometimes more intrigued with mind manipulation than meaningful effort to resolve conflicts, his oratorical flights of fancy often spun in and crashed.

To commemorate blunders, impassioned tirades, and attempts to sneak one over on colleagues, we legislators had a menagerie of mascots in the form of small figurines. An appropriate figurine would be placed on the offender's desk, usually in mid-speech. Most recipients would get the message and wind down their antics. Not John. Instead, whatever offense he was committing would be amplified in his apparent effort to win permanent possession of whichever trophy he'd been presented. Among these were the Tiger, the Fox, and the Blooper. Hellenthal's verbosity compelled me to conclude these did not quite cover all situations, so I proposed another.

> The low-frequency tongue of pure silver is not
> The type of a tongue we would tether.
> But *please* put a bung up in front of the tongue
> Made of flapping, high-mileage, whang leather!

Whereupon I presented John with the new trophy, a king-size thermos bottle cork.

Another attorney, Bill Irwin, had, as Rules chairman, apparently memorized every jot and tittle of Robert's Rules of Order. The slightest provocation would inspire in this Democrat from Seward an insufferable demonstration of his superior knowledge, often accompanied by scorn at those who, like myself, would in ignorance abuse protocol. Thus it was with gusto I presented him with another addition to our menagerie. This was occasioned when Irwin, after first vigorously protesting a piece of legislation, was forced by political expediency to vote in favor. The figurine presented to Waffling Willie was a bone china chicken.

> Along with the Blooper, Tiger, and Fox
> We now add the trophy contained in this box.
> And who's first to win this award? Why by golly
> It's none other than Irwin, the *new* Seward's Folly!

Three conservative Fairbanks Republican members of the House—Forbes Baker, Ed Baggen, and Jim Binkley—were known as the B Boys. They usually cast their votes as a bloc. One notable exception was a proposal to repeal the bounty on wolverines. Baker and Baggen reflected the public attitude of the time, which was to kill off all the "varmints." Binkley, however, favored repeal of the bounty.

In the process, Binkley crossed swords with Bob Blodgett, the prime advocate for the bounty. One day Blodgett brought a contingent of Native constituents to Juneau from his home district to attest to the importance of retaining the bounty. By the time he completed his impassioned floor address, one would have thought the entire economy of Northwest Alaska depended upon wolverine bounty payments. More amused than abused, Jim Binkley rose to counter Bob Blodgett's assertion in a manner I attempted to capture in verse.

We recall when the bounty was under the gun
Our sympathies Blodgett had just about won

By painting that critter the sly wolverine
As odious, wretched, corrupt, and obscene.

"Bounties paid for the hair of this pest
Support all my people in Alaska's northwest!"

In response Jim's incisors flashed white in the sun:
"Records show last year's wolverine take numbered just *one!*"

This revelation that hunters and trappers were hardly prospering from the wolverine bounty did not move the Legislature to scuttle it. All bounties were very popular back then, and lawmakers as a matter of survival were disinclined to be identified with an unpopular repealer.

DEMOCRAT WENDELL KAY, though brilliant, was nonetheless an attorney and therefore suspect among Republicans, whom he delighted in outmaneuvering. One prime example of his fancy footwork related to the always-controversial issue of legislative pay. We Republicans had introduced a bill in the House to cut back our salaries, which had been increased by the prior Democrat-controlled Legislature and sorely criticized by the electorate. In a remarkable display of political contortion, Kay, while berating Republicans for not proposing a more substantial cut, lauded Democrats for their staunch support of the new salary schedule.

A minor pay cut or none at all was the choice confronting the minority Republicans, who were never allowed to forget we were just that: the minority. We were assured that should we demand a substantial pay cut, none at all would occur. We Republicans once again displayed our lack of political smarts by choosing a small pay cut rather than none, thereby not only reducing our salaries but incurring the scorn of the public for backing down from our original position. Had we been a bit more astute we would have militantly stuck to higher principles—and been better paid for it.

Such chicanery was not confined to Democrats when it came to pay. Republican Jess Harris attempted to make points with constituents by sending his personal check to the state treasury, reimbursing it for what he piously pronounced was an excessive salary increase. This gesture, of course, cast a shadow on colleagues—myself included—who were less conscience-stricken with accepting their new level of remuneration. I didn't find it hard to rationalize my position.

I'm afraid that I must decline to decline
Any portion.of payment designated as mine.

For the electorate, while not endorsing cupidity,
Will forgive one of greed but never stupidity!

The legislator who moved me to greatest abuse of the muse was Clem Tillion, a Republican from Halibut Cove. A Brillo-haired, bronze-voiced commercial fisherman from the Kenai Peninsula, Tillion proved remarkably adept at hiding his brilliance behind a facade of outrageous conduct. I took advantage of his penchant for indiscretion by suggesting actions I was too timorous to undertake on my own. Sitting directly behind him, all it took was a knuckle in his back, accompanied by a whispered "Clem, why don't you . . . ?" to prompt Tillion to leap to his feet and perpetrate yet one more outrage.

Clem often was on the receiving end of indignant ripostes by those he abused. However, those who chose to tilt with him often found thrusts parried and themselves skewered. One prime example occurred when Jalmer Kertulla, occupying the House speaker's chair in 1968, upbraided Tillion for addressing the chair while in his stocking feet. Attorney Wendell Kay grasped this opportunity to state that Tillion was compelled to remove his shoes in order to think, because his brain was located in those extremities. This prompted quick rebuttal from Tillion, and here—providing for poetic license—is an encapsulation of what he said:

Attorneys, you'll note, never fail to stand
Lest their thinking be fully depleted

Due to the fact that a barrister's brain
Is constrained by the pressure when seated.

When Clem Tillion became president of the Senate in 1979, I provided him with a three-foot-long, twenty-pound gavel, along with the following note: "Should you ever wish to have a show of hands on a motion, remember, it always helps to have a few extras in your desk drawer." I signed the note "Great, great, great, great, great, great Uncle Genghis." Genghis Khan seemed to many to be Clem's role model. I'd hoped to accompany this note with a cadaver's hand, to be supplied by Clem's daughter, Martha, who was a medical student. Unfortunately all she could acquire was a finger, which I duly presented to Tillion.

Some asserted that crusty old Clem actually had the heart of a small boy and the brain of a genius—both of which he kept in a jar of formaldehyde on his mantle. The finger, being more portable, Clem often kept on his person, never knowing when he might put it to use. Such opportunity occurred as he had dinner one evening with hard-nosed Senate colleague Bill Ray. Ray noticed that Clem was toying something about on his plate with a fork. Ray's casual interest flared into green-gilled horror as he took a closer look after Clem asked: "Bill, did any of *your* hors d'oeuvres have nails on them?"

Along with giving Clem the finger, something many of his colleagues would have loved to do if they dared, I pointed out the prime qualification required of a presiding officer.

If you would sit in the president's chair
Bear one thing in mind, my friend:
There's more to the job than controlling the mob.
To forget this, some of us tend.

Now all of us know the job has some rewards
Like a sizable increase in salary.
And none can deny that it is the prime spot
For ogling girls in the gallery.

Yet while it is true that the job has some pros,
Don't *ever* lose sight of the cons
For that seat is the loneliest spot in the world
A fact which suddenly dawns

When one's forced to hold ever a dignified face
And cannot engage in such capers
As surreptitiously picking his nose
Or covertly reading the papers.

Such diversions are reserved for the peons down front
Who share not in your special doom.
For unnoticed these worthies can sneak out the door
To drink coffee or check the rest room.

You'll be on display all throughout the day,
For you sit in the public eye.
And that public demands that each session stands
Full measure, not one minute shy.

You can't leave your chair for just any whim
Or to satisfy nature's demands.
Delays cost too much, so tensely you sit,
Anxiously wringing your hands.

Yes, it takes more than leadership, firmness, and poise,
To climb to that rung of the ladder.
You'll need a reversible, semi-submersible,
Cat-gut and cast-iron bladder.

Presiding officers, of course, can do much to maintain decorum. However, most legislators will abide by certain protocols without directives from the chair. As a result, floor debate often resembles a stylized saraband in which bruised egos and heated tempers are obscured beneath phony posturing and insincere phrases such as "my esteemed colleague" or "the gentleman from Juneau." Such ploys usually are more subtle than the following suggestion that Tillion once made to a lawmaker :

I must admit yours is a very good bill
Well thought out, dynamic and vital.
But please accept this small amendment to same:
Delete everything after the title!

The pleasure Clem and I took in needling each other helped stitch together a friendship that, though I often strained its rough seams, remains in memory's wardrobe more warm down jacket than hair shirt. Clem's counsel, perverse sense of humor, and total candor helped keep my feet on deck instead of in my mouth. Clem usually gave as least as good as he got, and only once can I recall him at a loss for words. This phenomenon occurred during a trip to Japan while he and I were serving on the advisory committee to the International North Pacific Fisheries Management Council.

We were staying at a ryokan in Kyoto, and this traditional Japanese inn required us to conform to tradition. So, after bathing, everyone donned kimonos. Entering the dining area, we plodded in unshod feet to our respective places on tatami mats and did our best to squat Japanese style. This effort proved embarrassing to some, especially Harry Reitz, whose large frame, when folded in accordance with tradition, inclined his kimono to creep upward over long hairy shanks until it virtually nudged his navel. Noting his predicament, one little Japanese waitress shuffled over and, unfolding a large paper napkin, laid it discreetly over his lap.

Though Harry's already pink complexion suffused to russet, it could not match in splendor the glowing magenta of Clem's face when I summoned the concerned waitress and, securing another napkin from her, tore off a corner the size of a postage stamp and laid it like a miniature codpiece on Tillion's lap. At this all the waitresses came unglued and, hands obscuring giggles, had to retire briefly. Meanwhile, to Tillion's speechless discomfort, the rest of us almost choked on our sushi in laughter.

12 The right course

Rep. Hammond explains a point to his obviously
spellbound colleagues. Juneau, 1960

ASSEMBLING THE COGS and gears of a new state government machine almost fully occupied us at early legislative sessions, though other issues added spice, or sand, to proceedings that at best were not too well lubricated. Among the most persistent and provocative of these dealt with matters of "morality." Recognizing the difficulty of legislating morality, we often tried legislating *immorality.* Of course we did not do so blatantly. Instead we attempted to disguise one as the other. A prime example was a bill to make the legalization of gambling more palatable by restricting it to charitable or religious organizations. Church bingo was permissible. Casino bunco was not.

With mail order ministerial "ordinations" being readily available to those who wished to avoid seminary, I envisioned a whole new cadre of clerics emerging.

> Let us dust off the wheels of fortune
> And all innocent games of chance.
> If we're lucky we'll win their last penny
> And possibly even their pants.
>
> You can reap a rich harvest of goodies
> From the suckers you're entitled to hook,
> If you just put your collar on backward
> And wear a *benevolent* look.

Prior to statehood, gambling was illegal in Alaska, save for wagering on the Nenana Ice Classic. In this game, bettors purchased state-sanctioned tickets on which they guessed the time at which a clock-equipped tripod on the Tanana River near the town of Nenana would tip over as the ice went out during the annual spring breakup. Those guessing closest to the actual time won. Upon statehood, a special act legalized gambling only on the ice pool. Later, with legalization of "charitable" gambling, that pool has broadened and deepened. As might be expected, charity only gets to wade in it up to the ankles, while "entrepreneurs" and recipients of political contributions derived from the proceeds splash happily about at the deep end.

I've never been caught up in the mystique of gambling. Perhaps it's because I don't understand the rationale. For example, I can't quite grasp the idea of wagering on the team one hopes will win. Should that team lose, distress is doubly compounded. Were I a gambler, my inclination would be to vote *against* my favorite team. That way I might lose either pride or money, but not both!

For a number of years I followed the practice of never putting any money where my mouth was when it came to the Nenana ice pool. Each year I would pick a time, but not purchase a ticket. No doubt I was the only Alaskan praying his guess was wrong. Without fail my prayers were answered and I thereby profited—or at least avoided losses—from the ice pool to a far great degree than did 99 percent of those purchasing tickets. Despite my remarkable success, I no longer engage in that practice. As a victim of serendipity to whom good things seem to happen in spite of myself (such as the privilege of once governing the best state in the nation), I no longer dare chance it. It would be just my luck to pick the correct time.

As in any group, there were hypocrites in our legislative ranks. Most were covert in this regard, expressing outrage and moral indignation on the floor, while in private indulging in all manner of unseemly behavior. Opportunities for misconduct in Juneau during legislative sessions were, of course, facilitated by the absence of the prying eyes of constituents and, in many instances, one's family. A number of bars and the availability of a few "legislative groupies" beckoned some to explore primrose paths out of bounds back home.

One morning during an early opening session, Speaker Warren Taylor was distressed to find less than a quorum on the House floor. Where were the other members? Since this was the day after headlines had appeared announcing dismissal of an Anchorage jailer for taking advantage of several females in his custody, I believed I had an explanation.

> Where in the world have our lawmakers gone?
> Oh where the heck can they be?
> Could someone have bugged the inaugural flight
> And they're all garters up in the sea?
>
> No, the truth of the matter, my friends, is this:
> Though lacking permission from Speaker Taylor
> They've all sneaked off to Anchorage
> To apply for the job of jailer.

A proper, gray-haired, middle-aged legislator, Juneau Democrat Dora Sweeney, would often invite frustration on herself by attempting to legislate morality, seeking support amidst a group perceived to have little understanding of the word. Sweeney shared a desk with archconservative Forbes Baker, who often bickered with her over such issues as whether we should forgo *flogging* liberals before they were *hanged*. In response to Sweeney's attempt to pass a law clamping down further on drinking by teenagers by raising to nineteen the age at which they could legally drink, I made what I thought was an innovative proposal to address her concerns.

> If you really desire a decrease in crime,
> Abuse, assault, and corruption,
> Outrageous conduct, illicit birth,
> Mayhem and murderous ruction

The obvious way's not to pick on the kids,
Let them booze, while we get a bit bolder
And pass legislation denying strong drink
To all those who are nineteen or *older!*

JOHN NUSINGINYA, a Barrow Democrat, also took a stab at legislating morality when he introduced legislation dealing with B-girls, those provocatively clad females who served drinks in some establishments. Nusinginya felt this added attraction encouraged patrons to prolong their stay in bars, with an attendant increase in alcohol abuse. To reduce that enticement, he proposed a rigid dress code for the women.

After reviewing his bill carefully, I reached a startling yet intriguing conclusion. Amidst the several pages of boilerplate text, I'd found a speck of rust. Careful reading of sections describing prohibited attire revealed the only way B-girls could possibly comply was to wear nothing at all! While this startling revelation prompted an upwelling of support for the bill, over our strident protests Nusinginya withdrew it.

I initially got off on the wrong foot with John Holm, one of the few early-day Republican legislators. The occasion was the time he covertly slid a document from the drawer of his desk, passed it over to me, and whispered: "What do you think of this?" It was the first legislation he had planned to introduce; its subject, pornography.

After trying to decipher its many provisions, I was perplexed. The language describing what would be deemed illegal was so specifically clinical that I whispered back: "Tell me, John, does this mean you're for it or against it? The way it's written, you'd best forget the normal blue legislative binder and submit it in a plain brown wrapper."

Despite the confusion of some politicians when it comes to distinguishing among the moral, the amoral, and the immoral, most would have constituents believe *they* occupy the high ground while opponents wallow far below in a sea of corruption. "For motherhood and against sin!" was the essence of one particular campaign ad. I expressed my puzzlement in a poem.

When a candidate declares against sin
While endorsing motherhood
I must confess there is one thing
I've never understood.

Just what position should he take
On the most touchy matter
Of motherhood and sin alike
When the former results from the latter?

During long legislative sessions, I sometimes spent my time irreverently captioning photos.

Rep. John Rader, Democratic majority leader:
"Wait till those Republicans find out what this bill *really* does."

Rep. Bob Blodgett, no fan of Rep. Jim Binkley:
"You say Binkley may have perished in the Fairbanks flood?"

Rep. Dora Sweeney, who shared a desk with Rep. Forbes Baker:
"Forbes, you old devil, cut that out!"

Rep. John Holm, who sat next to me:
"When I push this little button, Hammond goes right through the roof."

Sen. Frank Pevatrovich to Governor Bill Egan:
"Psst, Bill, check your fly."

13 Wild waters

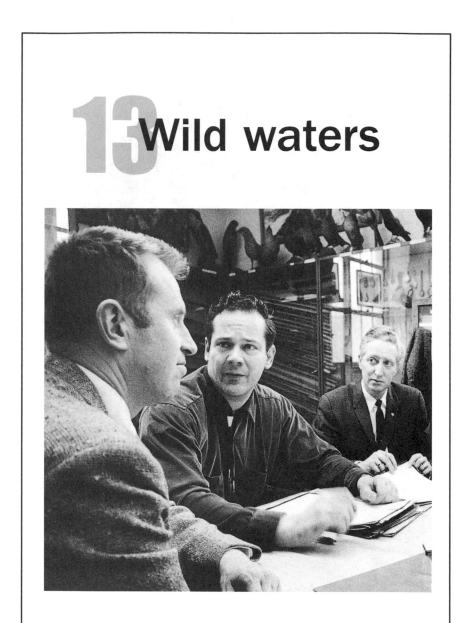

Our resource Committee met in the state museum amid other artifacts. Here I'm looking with alarm at legislative colleague Clem Tillion. 1962

DURING BILL EGAN'S FIRST TERM as governor, Alaska's financial condition remained precarious. While the rosy glow of potential oil development glimmered on the horizon, it was obscured by heat lightning and menacing storm clouds. Truth to tell, Alaska was almost bankrupt.

Of course, as is the wont of the party in power, reigning Democrats tried to put the best possible face on our condition. One who did not buy their propaganda was crusty conservative Bill Snedden, who was editor of the *Fairbanks News-Miner*. Snedden accurately assessed the financial difficulties facing Alaska in a scathing editorial alleging, at the very least, imprudence by Democrats. As a Republican and a member of the loyal opposition, I freely offered Democrats an appropriate response for them to make.

How dare this guy Snedden contend that we're broke
Just 'cause we're scratching a bare-bottom poke?
How naive can you get if you believe, sonny,
To be fiscally sound you gotta have money?

When someone laments that we're in fiscal peril
Just spit in their eye and roll out the pork barrel.
While we've et up the loins, the chops, and the jowls
There still remain bits of the bones and the bowels.

Just 'cause we're barefoot and out at the seat
Don't mean for a minute we ain't got it sweet.
So be happy to learn from what we Democrats say:
"You've been eatin' not beans, but the finest *filet!*"

At the end of Egan's first term, I reflected on some of the hazards confronting the ship of state as it sailed into the 1960s. After surviving its 1959 launch into statehood, Alaska was being painfully weaned from the federal teat. With the blessings of statehood also came obligations. Dwindling transitional monies had not been supplanted by income from predicted economic development. Consequently, Alaska rode into some pretty rough waters.

Financial concerns dominated early legislative sessions. Accordingly, especially coveted were seats on the finance committee, which writes the budget and parcels out pork. In the first year of statehood our total budget was only $50 million. While the budget grew fatter each year thereafter, it was but $143 million the year before receipt of our first oil treasure trove: $900 million from sale of leases on state lands in Prudhoe Bay. Prior to the Prudhoe lease sale, members of the finance committee were confronted with the task of stretching income to encompass outgo. Some years this was akin to trying to stuff a bowling ball into a toilet kit.

Each Legislature is addressed by not only the governor delivering his State of the State speech and budget message, but by our congressional delegation and by the chief justice of the state supreme court. These occasions presented an opportunity for these personages to lobby in behalf of their prime interests. Few did so more effectively than Egan's Chief Justice George Boney in pleading his case in 1960 for upgrading antiquated judicial facilities, which he deemed "more suitable for the Civil War era."

Despite our already strained budget, the chief justice's pleas were accommodated, but only after considerable grumbling by fiscal conservatives Forbes Baker and Don Harris, who felt additional funding should be accompanied by harsher criminal penalties. One suggested we consider adoption of a criminal code once proposed by Thomas Jefferson. Included therein was a provision requiring that those convicted of capital crimes be hung the following day, unless the conviction came on a Saturday. In such case Jefferson, mealy-mouthed liberal that he was, would permit execution to be delayed until Monday.

While Bill Egan easily won a second term as governor, upon its completion many were dismayed to learn he intended to run for a third. As president of the state's constitutional convention, Egan had supported inclusion of a gubernatorial limit of two consecutive terms in office. However, now he contended it was legally permissible for him to run again because he had not yet served two full terms. He was correct. Shortly before his second inauguration, Egan had fallen seriously ill and his next in command, Hugh Wade, assumed the duties of governor for several weeks.

Even many Democrat faithful were displeased with this attempt to end-run constitutional intent and, feeling the incumbent vulnerable, ran against him in 1967. Among these were Warren Taylor and Wendell Kay. On the Republican side were Bruce Kendall and Wally Hickel. Despite some Democratic disaffection, after the primary dust had settled, Egan emerged to confront Republican Wally Hickel in the general election. Kendall's loss to Hickel in the primary convinced him Republicans failed to recognize true talent, so he switched parties and became a sycophantic supporter of Egan, a man whom he had previously belittled unmercifully. Despite Kendall's blessing (some would say because of it) Egan was deposed in the general election by Hickel, who then served two years as governor until Richard Nixon appointed him Secretary of the Interior, and in 1969 Lieutenant Governor Keith Miller assumed the wheel.

DURING MY YEARS as a state lawmaker, a perennial issue was the length of the annual legislative session. Alaska's constitution provides for a forty-member House and a twenty-member Senate to meet annually at the state capitol in Juneau. At first, sessions lasted less than ninety days. We were paid a salary of three thousand dollars plus a daily allowance (per diem) of twenty-five dollars. Except for presiding officers, we had no staff, not even secretarial help. Committees met in any nook or cranny they could find, short of the men's room. I and the members of my resource committee met in the state museum amidst a number of other artifacts. Because legislators could not afford to do otherwise, when we arrived in Juneau we hit the deck running. Working many evenings and weekends, we usually adjourned within seventy days.

Then the sessions began to run longer. At first I found the increasing length confusing. After all, most fundamentals of government had been addressed. How could there possibly be, each year, dozens of issues we'd overlooked and now felt we must deal with? Obviously I'd not yet learned Parkinson's Law, which holds that "work expands to fill the time available." As legislators were provided additional "tools," we felt compelled to overuse them. Similarly, as dollars became more available, they had to be overspent.

I didn't have even a secretary until I became Senate majority leader and no aide or office until I became Senate president. Today even the newest minority member has at least a couple of aides, a secretary, a private office in Juneau, and another office back in the home district.

It is argued such emoluments are required to satisfy public demand for greater access to legislators. Yet increased access appears instead to have *increased* public frustration. For example, few Alaskans seemed concerned initially with the remoteness of Juneau as the state capital. But as communications improved through teleconferencing, free phone lines, home-district offices, travel allowances, and acquisition of staff to deal with matters of concern to constituents, voter frustration expanded rather than shrunk. This was evidenced by growing support to move the capitol to "an area of greater population density and easier accessibility." In that regard I urge caution. After all, greater accessibility seems to actually increase voter frustration. Obviously, familiarity *does* breed contempt.

When I became a state senator, it seemed inconceivable to me that the Senate's business could not be concluded within three months. After several futile efforts to curb session length while in the minority, I naively thought that with Republicans in control, we would more quickly kill the "snake." To do so I proposed we simply pay no per diem, but instead a flat salary equivalent to what we would get in per diem for ninety days. Were we to sit longer, all expenses would come out of our hides. That effort fell flat.

I now have a far better plan that would not only drastically cut costs by reducing staff and workload, but would also lessen voter contempt while at the same time benefiting legislators.

In 1995, for example, the Legislature cost the state $30 million. I proposed we cut the Legislature's budget in half and divide the remaining half among the sixty legislators. In 1995, that would have amounted to a quarter-million dollars apiece, and that would be their *salary*. From this they would pay all expenses, including staff. What they chose not to spend on legislative costs, they could pocket. By so doing, not only would they benefit themselves but also would contribute greatly to the public good by confining their legislative efforts to matters of consuming importance. With my plan implemented, I suspect we'd see sessions of no more than two weeks duration every other year.

Or maybe we should just go back to another proposal I once floated.

I've a new plan to shorten the session
Which some may think a bit crude:
Let's pass a bill that requires
All sessions be held in the nude

Upon the capitol lawn each day
Commencing January four.
(I bet that few would *stand* to demand
the privilege of the floor.)

Instead we'd cower in our seats
And not debate the issues
Lest we expose the gallery
To a glimpse of tender tissues.

I'm sure that some would like this ploy
With all its subtle facets
For we'd *have* to cut the budget
Once we'd frozen all our assets.

14 The privateers

Here's one of the lobbyists. Over time, I learned
they had another side.

BEFORE I SET FOOT in the state Legislature, I was warned to beware of lobbyists. So beguiling were these creatures alleged to be, that if I didn't remain constantly alert, they would undermine my moral principles, perhaps even cause a complete collapse of character.

Representative Jamie Fisher seemed especially alarmed by the lobbyists' evil influence. Embarking early on a crusade against the species, this Anchorage Democrat eloquently depicted them as a craven, reptilian blight that, if tolerated at all, should at least be gagged, shackled, and branded. Cited among the lobbyists' most curious and dastardly deeds was an alleged practice of making legislative payoffs by covertly passing funds through the transoms of hotel room doors. Fisher urged such activities be curbed by requiring some means of instant identification of lobbyists. But I already knew how to identify them.

> Just how can one tell a lobbyist
> From your garden-variety fiend?
> Does he have three horns, a single red eye,
> Or two noses of emerald green?
>
> Or are they often sweet innocent types
> Who, even as thee or me,
> Will cheat if they can on their income tax
> Or steal your teeth for a fee?
>
> There's one certain way to distinguish this breed
> Be they ever so ugly or handsome:
> Be assured they'll be wearing Adler elevated shoes
> So they can easily reach over a transom.

At first I viewed lobbyists with nervous suspicion. However, when after several weeks not one had approached me, I started to question their reputation. If they engaged in scurrilous activities, they certainly hid them from me. During my twenty years in public office, not once did a lobbyist attempt to subvert me—even though I always left my transom wide open, just in case.

None even tried to buy my dinner, much less my vote. While I'd like to think this indicated their conclusion I was not susceptible to blandishments, it may be they simply felt me so ineffectual as to not warrant massaging. Actually, I often found lobbyists to be fonts of information helpful in understanding complex issues. For that matter, somewhat to my surprise, virtually all lobbyists turned out to be exceptionally personable and, if tainted, able to successfully camouflage corruption.

One of the most personable and talented was Don Dicky, a lobbyist for the Alaska State Chamber of Commerce. Don combined exuberant energy with exceptional wit. As a master of ceremonies he was in constant demand and without peer. Each year, Democratic legislators sponsored a dinner for which Dicky and I were usually asked to serve as co-emcees. This seemed curious, since we were both Republicans and the event gave us the rare opportunity to not only probe the soft underbelly of political sacred cows, but also to verbally depants those trying to milk them. At one such function I tried to reduce any affront to individuals I might target by announcing:

"In the past I've been accused of abusing everyone in the audience. So tonight, in penance, I'm going to depart from past practice, and insult but a select few. Selectees should be aware I only insult those I happen to like, so of them I wish to request a favor. It's hard to insult a man to his face, looking directly into his outraged, beady red eyes, so I'd appreciate it if when you hear your name you have the common decency to crawl under the table."

After a small oil spill in Cook Inlet, I penned this "Oil Lobbyist's Lament" as if from an industry apologist.

Oh why, oh why, must it happen to us,
Each time things simmer down,
A slick shows up in some waters
Where an abundance of birds are found?

You can bet your boots almost every time
It will be our damnable luck:
We strike a gusher, then someone finds
A floundering, well-oiled duck!

And though some scoff or may not know,
We really do lament
Pollution of what's termed by some
"Our pristine environment."

We'd stop every spill where seabirds abound
If we could have our druthers,
For it drastically lowers the price of crude
To have to strain out all those feathers.

Members of the media probably have no greater penchant for evil than lobbyists or other members of society, just greater opportunity. This is particularly true of reporters covering legislative sessions. Privy to many a behind-the-scene power play, they're often able to influence its outcome. Moreover, intense study of legislative issues induces the smug, and not unfounded, assumption that they know more about what's going on than does the average legislator. At their discretion the public is permitted insight—or held in ignorance. Such fosters a heady sense of power.

Not surprisingly, most members of the fourth estate hold politicians in something less than reverence. By contrast, most public figures hold members of the media, if not in high esteem, at least in some degree of apprehensive awe and are inclined to handle them accordingly. Forced to endure hours of numbing bombast each session, reporters are expected to sift nuggets from a morass of clinkers, then smelt them into some semblance of sense. That they frequently fail is not surprising, since often more heat than light is generated in the process. What *is* surprising is that otherwise reasonably normal human beings would long endure this work for the small salary and attendant indignities. Few did. As a consequence, a steady stream of reporters came and went.

While most politicians feel their oratorical gems often metamorphose into garbage when digested by the media, one reporter, Eve Reckley, gained both affection and esteem by frequently reversing that procedure.

Eve Reckley is a naive gal who hasn't learned the art
Of quoting out of context, thereby tearing us apart.

Instead she lets one have his head and gallop any way
He chooses 'cross the landscape of "The Topic for Today."

Then she will pick a bridle path which delicately shuns
Those comments, which instead of pearls, resemble more horse buns.

I love you, Eve, for while once I really used to dread it,
Your interviews most often read much better than I said it.

In fairness to the press, I must admit my oratory was sometimes so convoluted that interpretation presented a formidable challenge.

My arguments almost always are
Better than my opponent's, by far.
Often they surprise even me
With their brilliance, logic, and clarity.

Yet somehow in transit between brain and lip
My words seem unable to endure the trip.
They come out all backward and upside down
And instead of a genius I sound like a clown.

It's not really because my mind is slow
Nor that I am simply too dumb to know
Up from down, or north from south.
Rather I've a brilliant brain—but a stupid mouth!

From the advent of statehood, Alaska's two largest papers, the *Anchorage Times* and the *Anchorage Daily News,* squared off on almost every major issue. Bob Atwood, editor of the *Times,* was a blatant booster of any proposed development project; seemingly the more destructive, the better. Thus he championed such boondoggles as Rampart Dam, the use of atomic devices to indent coastlines where Mother Nature had thoughtlessly neglected to establish natural harbors, and relocation of the capitol from Juneau to a new "Brasilia" some seventy-five miles north of Anchorage in a semi-wilderness area. By contrast, Kay Fanning, editor of the *News*, expressed either caution or contempt for many projects favored by Atwood.

Initially the *Times* printed a laudatory editorial or two on my behalf. However, when I opposed Rampart Dam, atomic landscaping, and the tankering of oil through Alaska's pristine waters I incurred Atwood's wrath. His subsequent editorial blasts served to trigger an imprudent response of my own, and I had fun with the fact that the editorials appeared to violate Alaska law limiting "in kind" contributions to political candidates.

When we saw three editorials in Atwood's *Anchorage Times*
Scourging me as an environmentalist and accusing me of crimes

Such as advocating cautious growth and asking questions *first*
I must admit that my response was to fear the very worst.

But Bob's editorials *won* me points, according to some readers.
(Seems his backfires often boost election of our leaders.)

His diatribes and tantrums serve to make Alaskans mad.
"If Atwood hates your guts," I'm told, "you can't be all that bad."

Thus could his editorials, since they *helped* the Hammond cause,
Be deemed "in kind " contributions under our disclosure laws?

Would we then be made to list them and to estimate their worth?
Was Bob deep in troubled waters, or simply in the surf?

What's an Atwood editorial worth? Could it be five hundred dollars?
If so, then Bob's in trouble; I can already hear the hollers:

"Hey! The limit's just one thousand bucks, but he's donated fifteen hundred.
So let's slap him in the slammer for the fact that he so blundered."

But really, folks, we have no case, not even cause for cussing.
For who'd believe an Atwood editorial worth more . . . than absolutely *nothing*.

Appearances on radio or TV shows hosted by members of the media provided legislators the opportunity to either soar, or crash. One who derived satanic satisfaction from salting the tail feathers of political pigeons, thereby inducing stalls, was Herb Shainlin. I knew him well—and still liked him.

What lies behind Herb Shainlin's mask?
Is he just what meets the eye:
A boorish, ribald ogre?
Or a sweet and charming guy?

I for one have had the chance
To probe and pry and peer
Behind that cynical facade,
That Mephisto beard and leer

To where the *real* Herb Shainlin lives
Hidden largely out of sight.
And learned, by George, his critics . . .
They're absolutely right!

One other thing I learned from Herb–
no "if," "and," "but," or "maybe"–
I now know just exactly
What became of Rosemary's baby!

And just in case those words did not sufficiently burnish Herb's image, I later offered a sequel.

When Shainlin did duty on Channel 13
It seemed every night might have been Halloween

As he fiendishly, sometimes without being asked,
Would remove for a moment his outlandish mask

And one found that behind it there beat a soft heart:
Yours! Which he'd torn out and was gnawing apart!

A new upper berth

A broken tie vote put me into the hot seat as Senate president when an unknown Democrat defector switched votes in a secret ballot. Juneau, 1970; Elaine Mitchell photo

I WAS BEATEN for reelection to my House seat in 1965 by Joe McGill, a Democrat from Dillingham, another political opponent who later became a good friend. When I returned two years later to the Legislature, I was a member of the Senate. Joe was still in the House, and we had a chance to work together on projects for our district.

During my first campaign for the Senate it appeared I had little likelihood of winning as a Republican in the new Democrat-dominated Senate district, so I tried a different approach. In the villages of South Naknek and Nondalton, which I had never carried during three previous successful runs for the House, I made this pitch: "You folks fault me for not getting projects you requested, like roads and airfields. The difficulty has been trying to extract funds from a Democrat administration which knows you're going to vote Democrat regardless of whether or not you get those projects and failure to do so will be blamed on Republican Hammond.

"Why don't you shake them up as Nulato once did? Instead of voting Democrat as usual, one election they voted solidly Republican. To woo them back to the Democrat fold, they finally got the new school and airfield they had asked for in the past. Why not try the same ploy?" They did, and I was elected to the Senate.

In response to my plea that we build the roads and schools requested by Nondalton, South Naknek, and a third village, Manakutuk, or else they would surely return to the Democrat camp, Governor Hickel's chief of staff, Wally Kubely, told me: "Hammond, you bandit. We're going to give you two-thirds of our off-highways money and build those schools, roads, and airfields in all three villages. You should never again lose one of their votes."

Come the next election in 1970, I lost all three (but won the election anyway). "What goes on here," I wondered about the three villages. Enlightenment came when I learned who was on the beach directing traffic when bulldozers and building materials were barged ashore. Not Hammond. To this day most villagers credit Joe McGill for obtaining those projects.

My indoctrination into the Senate was enlightening. For one thing I quickly learned that distinctions between the House and Senate were not as clear-cut as I had imagined back when I was a member of the House.

When I served in the House it was clear to all in it
Most fumbling and bumbling occurred in the Senate.

But things seemed to change as I moved up the ladder:
I grew a bit older and wiser and sadder.

Now in the Senate I find one thing is true:
Some things *never* change, nor give way to the new.

I've learned, for example, that the idiots all
Are *still* found at the *other* end of the hall!

One notable distinction between House and Senate was the means by which members were called into session. In the House a no-nonsense buzzer summoned members to the floor. The Senate, however, opted for something that was deemed more aesthetically appropriate to its lofty station.

In days of old when men were bold
And they were called to battles,
The summons came from bugles
Blasting notes like "Boots and Saddles."

Or to some other call to arms
They'd into the onslaught hurl;
Perhaps the boom of ram's horn, drums,
Or bagpipe's wild skirl.

But nowadays things have changed a lot,
Sad comment on the times.
The Senate's call to arms? Notes struck,
Ethereally, on the chimes.

Wafting gently down the hall
This sound graciously enjoins
Us in the Senate to gird up
Our legislative loins.

With these dulcet tones we feel compelled
To adopt a pace which hints
Less of determined manly stride
And more of dainty mince.

Someday, I fear, those chimes will cause
A couple in our band
To embarrass us by skipping
To the chambers hand in hand.

During my first years in the Senate, that body was presided over by John Butrovich, a Fairbanks Republican. Revered by his colleagues, Butrovich was a no-nonsense Senate president who wielded his gavel with absolute fairness. So powerful was his presence that with but a word or facial expression he could subdue the most obstreperous member or change a crucial vote.

John's regal bearing and rocklike integrity evoked neither ridicule nor heated rebuttal. Preferring to let others grandstand, he would instead cut through rhetoric and whip the body into compliance with his position. Of course, John had an unfair advantage. He was the only member who *looked* like a senator.

Under Butrovich the second in command, as majority leader, was Brad Phillips, a Republican from Anchorage, an articulate and polished performer well-versed in legislative procedure. Between them they ran a tight ship, save for those infrequent occasions when, because of Phillips' absence, I was compelled to step in. By virtue of tenure rather than talent I had been propelled into the role of majority whip. Never one to pay rapt attention to business when more important considerations came up, I often found it difficult to compose verse or complete a crossword puzzle while obligated to oversee business taking place on the floor.

The crew over which Butrovich presided included potentially mutinous types that few others could have kept under control. Among them were the bombastic Bob Blodgett; Bill Ray, who could be even more irascible than Blodgett; archconservative Vance Phillips; even archer conservative Clyde (C. R.) Lewis; ultraliberal Nick Begich; a batch of lawyers that included John Rader, Chancy Croft, and Joe Josephson; Bill Poland, a fellow big-game guide who deplored neckties almost as much as I did; fellow conservationist Bob Palmer, who was often at odds with ardent pro-developers such as Frank Harris, Carl Brady, Ron Rettig, and Jack White; and Jan Koslosky, who like some of the rest of us always gave the impression he'd rather be fishing.

This colorful and divergent group was inclined to orate at length on almost all issues. Interminable debate prompted me to formulate Hammond's Law.

> Now every issue has a black side,
> As well as one that is white.
> And it takes lots of time, as all of us know
> To prove that *both* shadings are right.
>
> "Hammond's Law" clearly applies
> Whenever we follow this course:
> "The less the subject's significance,
> The more the amount of discourse."
>
> Thus we may reach few conclusions
> But certainly through the haze
> It's clear how we legislators can cram
> Two weeks hard work into *ninety* days.

While progress was exceedingly slow at the beginning of each legislative session, a curious phenomenon always occurred at the end as legislators raced to finish up.

At the start of every session and despite the public howl
There seems to be a stricture in the legislative bowel.

Yet at the *close* of every session, in spite of all their faults,
The bills are urged, processed, and purged as if by dose of salts.

In the wake of one exhausting debate I finally offered the following system of stereotyped, preformulated speeches as a means of expediting Senate business.

In order to speed up legislative affairs,
Mr. President I humbly propose
That stereotype speeches for our special use
Be numbered, and thus we can close

Off debate before we've grown numb,
As spring fades to summer, then autumn
And all we have to show for the session's
The callus we've grown on the bottom.

Speech number 1, in support of a bill,
Is a reasonable explanation
Couched in legal terms, full of logic and sense,
Of some twenty minutes duration.

Speech number 2 would then be the response,
We might even present it in rhyme.
This time legal logic is twisted about,
As is done now much of the time.

Speech number 3 is a popular one
And its use creates a sensation.
Hold breath till face reddens, then leap up and shout "3!"
To your credit: ten minutes of outraged indignation.

Speech number 4 is a wonderful one:
Obscure references used with great skill
Carefully tailored to hide the fact
That the speaker has not read the bill.

Speech number 5, my favorite I think,
Is designed to reduce in one spasm
A composed opponent to a speechless mass
Of quivering protoplasm

By questioning motives, integrity, brains
and, as distress slowly increases,
Even delving into the sanctity of
Your antagonist's oil leases!

By substituting speech numbers, the average debate
Which takes hours to finally get through
Could be telescoped down to a fraction of that
And be done in a minute or two.

A colorful style was as commonplace as controversy in many early senators. One who supplied an abundance of both was blustery Bill Ray. As chairman of the finance committee, Ray wielded immense power. Since he controlled the purse strings, members generally caved in to his blatant efforts to sink his hometown, Juneau, under the weight of capital improvements. While a caustic curmudgeon, Ray could also be most generous and helpful; hence few senators chanced incurring his displeasure, as I did in this rhyme.

I made the mistake of calling Bill Ray
A boondoggling, high-handed free-booter.
"I'm not either!" said he. "I don't do anything *free*.
What's more, I'm a gracious straight shooter.

"Can I help if you guys stick your beady red eyes
In front of my straight-shooting gun barrel?
Remember, it's every dog for himself.
Lift your leg on Bill Ray at your peril!"

But should Bill then pitch one a penny or two
Which he does with a great deal of charm
For a brief moment you may almost forget
The death grip he's got on your arm!

16 High winds

My conservationist leanings often had me chewed on by special
interests more concerned with the buck than the biota.
1975; Scott Foster photo

IN THE MID-SIXTIES the environmental movement began to send tremors through Alaska's political landscape. Many political chameleons, to soften their image as blatant damn-the-torpedoes, full-speed-ahead developers, adopted some protective coloration. I gave voice to one of these types in verse.

Hey! Look at me, folks, I'm really concerned
With the environment, for I've discerned

That *here* lie the votes in these troubled days
And a conservationist's stance is the one that pays.

So I stand 'fore the public in tight tennis shoes,
Drinking in nature instead of just booze.

Bird-watching glasses slung 'round my throat
Not Hefner, *Thoreau's* the guy I now quote.

Yes, I'll support conservation with vigor and pluck
(Unless, of course, it should cost *me* a buck.)

Environmentalists and developers often clashed, and no more so than at Fish and Game Board hearings. Here, pure biological considerations were often accommodated to the political. Since virtually every Alaskan professed great expertise on such matters, these sessions were often prolonged and bloody.

The debates of those times continue yet today on such subjects as wolf management, fishing of intermingled salmon stocks, hunting antlerless moose, and having a hunting season on musk oxen. I tried to cover all the bases in a bit of speculative verse after President Nixon, whose Interior Secretary at the time was Alaska's own Wally Hickel, presented a pair of musk oxen to China.

President Nixon, we're told, sent to Chairman Mao
One musk ox bull and one musk ox cow.

And along with those beasts, in return for his folly,
Dick sent that old ox expert Wally

To tidy up things in the wake of the pair
To curry their hides and sweep out their lair.

I can hear Wally shout as he leaves for Cathay:
"Hey, all you guys, there's a better way

"To shatter the might of the communist horde,
Just let me appoint them a fish and game board.

"And six months later we'll find with any luck
(I'll bet a myopic mallard to their peeking duck)

"That Chairman Mao has thrown in the towel
After being exposed to the collective howl

"Of 3 billion experts on fish and game
Looking for anyone who they can blame.

"And if that's not enough, we next could turn loose
Lowell Thomas astride an antlerless moose.

"Leading a wolf pack, and to compound the jolt,
Dumping into their waters mixed salmon smolt."

The coup de grace he'd give, when after crossbreeding
Two mismated creatures, he'd then start reseeding

The whole of China with bastards to which we gave birth
By crossing the Chamber of Commerce with Friends of the Earth.

ONE OF THE MOST CONTROVERSIAL issues confronting legislators was the proposed detonation of a atomic device on Amchitka Island
in 1971. The project, named Cannikan, was designed to see if it was possible to use atomic explosions to create harbors or to slice roadways through
glaciers. Cannikan was ardently favored by pro-development factions and
opposed with equal ardor by environmentalists, who feared harm to endangered species.

The fact that the Atomic Energy Commision seemed so reassuring
about the proposed blast and appeared so certain about what would happen got me wondering.

My cohort Clem Tillion has an explanation of why I've managed
to achieve some degree of popularity after a rough start. "Very simple,"
Clem says. "You confuse everybody into thinking you support their position on issues. Cannikan was a perfect example. The joint resolution you
drafted on it convinced both sides you were in accord with their views."

He referred to my effort to bring closure to a deadlocked Legislature,
which was almost split down the middle and hence afraid to take any position
on this matter. Day after day we were thumped to the left in the morning by
the Anchorage Daily News, which ardently opposed the blast, only to be rocked
back to the right by a wallop from the afternoon Anchorage Times, which with
equal ardor favored the program.

As we floundered about, unwilling to express ourselves on this heated
issue, other crucial state business went unaddressed. As majority leader of
the Senate it fell upon me to try to expedite matters. To resolve the impasse I
wrote a resolution that I first took to Lowell Thomas who, along with every
Alaskan conservationist, vigorously opposed Cannikan.

After reading it, Lowell enthused: "I agree wholeheartedly. You have my support."

I then took it to real estate developer Jack White, a firm Cannikan advocate. "That's fine with me," Jack said. "Introduce it and let's get this thing out of our hair."

I received similar encouragement from both sides of the aisle and the resolution passed, unanimously.

The following day the *Anchorage Times,* in preparation for its publication that evening, came up with a headline that trumpeted "Legislature Supports Cannikan Project." Meanwhile the morning *Anchorage News* headlined "Legislature Opposes Cannikan Blast." This compelled the *Times* to snatch up their first edition before it hit the streets and put out a second, with a headline that read something like: "Legislature Didn't Know What It Was Doing on Cannikan."

What *I* thought I was doing was simply predicating legislative support or opposition on whether reasonable conditions were met to which all parties could agree. Since both sides were assured such conditions could or should be met, despite being extremely unlikely, they found it hard to take exception to those conditions. Tillion's bemused response to the confusion: "Hammond, you did it again. You said absolutely nothing—but beautifully." Eventually an atomic device was detonated on Amchitka, but with such controversial results that other such planned experiments were canceled.

While I really don't intend to bamboozle listeners, sometimes my convolutions apparently present a maze through which they are unable to stumble. Lee Jordan, editor of the Eagle River *Star,* once wrote that the first time he heard me speak, he was quite impressed. He said he sat there nodding in agreement and taking notes. "Then I'd listen a little more, scratch out what I'd written, and make further notes. This went on until my head was spinning." Later he attended another Hammond presentation with a couple of legislators. While all agreed with what I had to say, later none could agree as to just what that *was.*

CERTAINLY THE MOST PAINFUL and divisive issue to confront legislators in the 1960s was abortion. While most considered themselves either pro-choice or right-to-life, it became evident almost none were truly one or the other. Few deeming themselves pro-choice advocated *complete* choice: this is, a woman's right to terminate pregnancy for any reason at any time up to severance of the umbilical cord. Similarly, few but the most zealous right-to-lifers opposed *all* abortions, even in cases of rape or incest or when the life of the mother was at stake.

Accordingly, most were in fact *limited* pro-choicers. Once an exception is made, even, say, for incest or rape, one departs the ranks of true right-to-life advocacy and accepts a small list of "choices." Though such choices may number only two, a list of choices is a list of choices, no matter how abbreviated.

Many find it confusing that some people, asserting abortion to be murder, can argue it is, however, permissible to take the life of the innocent end-product of rape or incest. Similarly, why would true pro-choice advocates deny a woman the choice of terminating a pregnancy for any reason through the third trimester? At what point does killing an unwanted fetus translate from humane to homicidal?

Ardent conservative Vance Phillips and liberal Nick Begich were in bitter opposition on almost every issue. Abortion was no exception. While there is certainly nothing humorous about the issue, the hypocrisy and inconsistency displayed by legislators agonizing over abortion prompted me to a few wry observations, starting with this one about Vance Phillips.

> Vance is having a little bill whipped up
> Which should prompt wondrous reception.
> It makes illegal the interruption of pregnancy,
> Not just after, but *prior* to conception.

> Thus, girls, no more refusal on any grounds.
> So don't bother to shriek, slap, or claw.
> For *not* to consent will, of course, constitute
> A flagrant violation of law!

In the desire to give equal offense to both sides, I suggested where Nick Begich's position might be heading.

> Nick has a plan that a few find attractive:
> He'd make some abortions *retroactive.*

> He'd chose certain birth dates and then he'd apply
> The measure selectively; so pity the guy

> Whose birthday just happens to fall by mere chance
> On the same date as–would you believe–Senator Vance?

17 Treasures unearthed

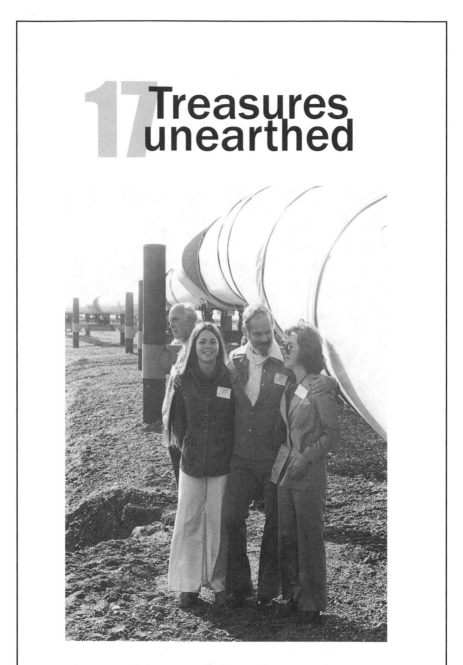

On a tour of the trans-Alaska pipeline at Prudoe Bay with
my wife, Bella, and daughter Heidi. 1978

DURING THE SIXTIES the Legislature fumbled about, trying to determine just how many feathers we could pluck from oil's high-flying golden goose without causing it to migrate or crash-land. Our initial mistake was to establish an unrealistically low oil severance tax of but 1 percent. This was done in hope of persuading oil companies "to come to Alaska and get their feet wet." Once having done so, however, some members of the industry complained we later opened the sluices and attempted to drown them in legislation that repeatedly changed the rules of the game.

In that regard I agreed they were treated unfairly, though I doubted they were yet overtaxed. Our mistake was to initially undertax them at 1 percent. Instead we should have first set a very high severance tax and then trimmed it as conditions demanded. Perhaps rather than 1 percent we should have started at, say, 99 percent. Then we could have lowered it to 98 percent, then 97 percent, and so forth. Once we started to get vibrations, we would have known we were approaching "the ballpark." Instead, we first let oil interests load all the bases, and then we tried to beanball and double-play them.

With the advent of oil development coinciding with newly emerging environmental awareness, Alaskans were inundated with counsel from folks living elsewhere who were determined to save us from ourselves. Many Alaskans resented this interference and responded with bumper-sticker slogans such as: "We Don't Give a Damn How They Did It Outside" and "Let the Bastards Freeze in the Dark."

As oil activity expanded and the money started rolling in, Alaska changed inexorably. Along with the good came plenty of bad, as development in the views of many started eroding the Alaskan style of life and endangering the environment. So, what was one who came up here to escape the environmental degredation found elsewhere to do?

I'll take all that big fat money
You say will come to me
And seek out some new "Alaska"
Somewhere beyond the sea.

And I really must be going soon
For I'm a rough and ready guy
Who wants to take his cut and run . . .
Before he starts to cry.

Such sentiments got me branded a flaming environmentalist, a charge which to some Alaskans was only slightly less reprehensible than child molestation. Of course, I brought much criticism on myself by irreverently twisting the tails of virtually every sacred cow, while rudely exposing just whose hands were fondling the udders.

One of my major concerns was over the danger of permitting loaded oil tankers to travel Alaskan waters. In 1964, some twenty-five years before the *Exxon Valdez* disemboweled itself on the rocks of Bligh Reef, I speculated on such possibility in a bit of satirical poetry that included such stanzas as the following.

Remember how lousy things used to be?
Before we had oil, fish cluttered the sea.
And Cook Inlet's waters were coffee-hued
Instead of the shimmering sheen of crude.

The poem was printed in virtually every Alaska newspaper as well as several Outside, including the *Sierra Club News*. It seems my old crony Clem Tillion had, unbeknownst to me, sent them all a copy. It came as no surprise that I had affronted the oil companies, along with the Chamber of Commerce, Governor Egan, the Republican Party, and most decent, as well as indecent, Alaskans.

As Alaska stepped over the threshold into an era of expanded, resource-oriented industrial development, we often stumbled and fell flat when it came to safeguarding important values against ravaging by the twin gods of Progress and Development. Sins committed in their names have been legion and monstrous, while those committed in the name of conservation, few and ephemeral at worst.

In 1969 the sale of oil leases in Prudhoe Bay engulfed Alaska in more money than had flowed into state coffers during all years prior to statehood combined: $900 million! Most politicians felt they had entered Nirvana. With all that money to spend, there seemed no more need to say "No!" Proposals to spend the windfall soon outnumbered dollars available.

Fortunately, before it could all be squandered, a series of legislative seminars were set up by the Brookings Institute think tank to explore potential uses of the money and invite public input. The Brookings Conference, held in Anchorage, was well attended. Only after a number of plans for the money were set forth did we in the Legislature *then* squander the money—or, at least so it seemed to most Alaskans. During these seminars many innovative proposals surfaced; fortunately most floundered.

Most participants at the conference, of course, were intent upon using our newfound fortune to fashion the future according to their own blueprint. On the one hand were those who envisioned a state where economic development sped ahead unimpeded. Others, particularly those who had come to Alaska to escape environmental degradation elsewhere, were intent upon erecting roadblocks. All, not surprisingly, cloaked their arguments in terms designed to obscure any suggestion of self-interest.

The theme of the conference appears to be this:
Which destiny shall be ours?
A multitude reaching for subway straps?
Or a handful who reach for the stars?

An amazing array of new ideas and inventions were trotted out by the Brookings staff to enlighten us about the future. These wonders were paraded before us in the hope we would shuck our gold rush mentality and prepare for the twenty-first century by investing our wealth imaginatively. One of the most provocative ideas concerned recycling. A conferee produced a paper outlining research on recycling newsprint into a high protein food additive. I immediately speculated how this breakthrough might affect my prime critics, newspaper editors Bob Atwood and Lew Williams.

They say there's a wondrous day coming
In nutrition when we will crush
Old newsprint and sprinkle it over
Our microorganic mush.

Now won't it be then satisfying
After years of indigestible blurbs
To know that editors Atwood and Williams
will at long last be eating their words!

Fearful that the $900 million windfall might appear squandered if there was nothing tangible to show for it, several proposals were made to invest in projects that would be lasting testimony to Alaska's good fortune. I agreed, and offered my own suggestion:

Just what should we do
With that nine hundred million?
Why, enshrine in gold plate
The outhouse of Clem Tillion.

What better symbol of progress
From rags to riches?
Demanding homage from all
When they lower their britches

And then leap to attention
From the painful threshold
Of a metalized seat
That is blistering cold!

Later on, a few of us, including Governor Miller, urged establishment of a prudent investment account from which only the earnings could be spent. However, so great were the state's needs, wants, and demands that this counsel went unheeded. All $900 million was quickly sopped up. Political expediency carried the day when legislators stared hungrily at this fortune and decided to spend most of it on municipal revenue-sharing or on appeasing one special interest or another.

Much of the money went to help local governments fund education and other services. Hence benefits to the people came hidden in the form of dollars saved in municipal taxes that would have been required had these programs not been funded with state revenue. Most citizens failed to understand how the oil money was helping them, and efforts by legislators to point out how much constituents were saving in local taxes went almost unnoticed. So dim was perception by voters of benefits received that Governor Keith Miller earned few brownie points. Come the 1971 election, Bill Egan once more was governor.

THE PROPOSED ALASKA OIL PIPELINE was a dominant issue during Egan's third term. At one point he proposed the state build it. The idea of ownership was later rejected, to be supplanted by debate over a pipeline route to carry Prudhoe Bay oil to market. Most Alaskans wanted an all-Alaska route that would deliver crude oil to the port of Valdez. However, a number of studies indicated both the state and the nation would make greater profit from oil piped directly into the thirsty Midwestern marketplace, rather than to Valdez, from whence it would be hauled by tanker to the Lower 48, with some shipped eastward through the Panama Canal to Gulf refineries. The profit differential was due to the fact that severance taxes are determined by the wellhead price, less transportation costs. Only if oil were sold in the Asian market and carried in less-expensive foreign bottoms did the return to the state and feds approximate that which both would receive if oil were piped across Canada into the Midwest.

This consideration was among several that prompted environmental groups and commercial fishermen to threaten a lawsuit that could delay pipeline construction and escalate costs. Among other factors were the recently passed Environmental Protection Act, which required study of alternative pipeline routes; the fact that a Canadian route would avoid the danger of tankering oil through Alaska's pristine marine waters; and allegations of rights-of-way violation.

In light of these threats I felt it prudent to assure we touched all legal bases and were aware of the comparative economics. Toward this end, I introduced a Senate resolution that cited these concerns and urged evaluation of alternative routes and clarification of rights of way. I did not advocate a Canadian route. However, had I known then what I know now, I would have done so—and thus would no doubt have committed political harí-karí, so blinded were most Alaskans by those likely to profit more from the all-Alaska route.

As I mentioned, only if oil went to Asian markets via foreign bottoms would the state earn as much revenue as from a trans-Canadian pipeline. My assumption, along with that of virtually everyone else involved, was that Alaska oil *would* be shipped to Asia. Only in that case would a port in Valdez make comparative economic, if not environmental, sense. Japanese buyers asserted they had already negotiated to purchase Alaska oil. The major remaining argument for a Canadian route was avoidance of tankering, apparently insufficient cause for most Alaskans to even permit a discussion of alternatives to an Alaska route.

This I discovered upon introduction of my resolution in 1970. En route to the Senate floor I encountered Bob Palmer, one of the most intelligent members of the Senate. Bob read my resolution and signed on. Only when it hit the hopper did we realize we might have signed our political death warrants. To hear the reaction, you'd think we had shrieked an obscenity in church. We were pilloried in virtually every paper for daring to even *suggest* that an alternative route be evaluated.

Today that resolution seems the essence of reason since it warned precisely of what happened in the wake of our failure to meet legal requirements. Environmentalists sued; construction of the trans-Alaska pipeline was delayed a year and costs escalated from the original estimate of less than $1 billion to almost $10 billion. The subsequent *Exxon Valdez* oil spill prompted reassessment by many, as did later efforts to overturn the congressional prohibition on selling oil to Asian markets—part of the price paid to obtain the trans-Alaska route.

18Shanghaied

Hand on the good book, I'm sworn in as governor of Alaska.
Juneau, 1974

EVERY TEN YEARS the governor must construct a new legislative reapportionment plan to reflect population shifts. This gave Governor Egan the opportunity to devise a scheme that permitted him to accommodate friends and chastise opponents. He was entirely too partisan a Democrat to forgo doing precisely that. Egan's reapportionment plan put me head to head with popular Senator George Hohman, a Democrat from Bethel, the largest city within my new district. This was sufficient excuse to announce I did not plan to run again. Not only would Hohman have proved a formidable opponent, but also after twelve years in the Legislature I was bit jaded and looked forward to other pursuits. In the spring of 1972 I departed Juneau with no return intentions.

For the next two years I kept busy flying, guiding, commercial fishing, serving as manager/mayor of the Bristol Bay Borough, and reacquainting myself with my family. Reentering the political arena was the last thing I had in mind. Few were more surprised than I to find myself running for governor in 1974. I had been out of the Legislature for two years and missed the legislative process about as much as I would a chronic backache. I filed to run for governor only because a few folks succeeded in making me believe they thought I had made a commitment to do so if they, in turn, undertook efforts in behalf of my candidacy. Though I knew I had not made such a commitment, I lacked the courage to incur their wrath by not acceding.

Since I had but a 3 percent name identification with the public and was pitted in the Republican primary against previous governors Miller and Hickel—and, should I survive the primary, heaven forbid, I'd face Alaska's most popular politician, Bill Egan, in the general election—I was not at all worried about winning. With but a few thousand dollars in the campaign war chest I announced I would run only to the extent that funds were available and said I would spend not one dime of my own. With those stipulations I thought my candidacy might last a week before I could go home to the hills where most political observers and I felt I belonged.

Initially none laughed more loudly than I over the improbability of my candidacy, but after defeating Hickel handily in the primary, I started to sober up. What goes on here? Still, not to worry. Apparently many Democrats had crossed over in Alaska's open primary to vote for the weakest Republican opponent to face their man Egan, who had no serious opposition in his own party.

To my considerable surprise, polls showed I had a substantial lead over Egan for the general election. Then Egan and his lieutenant governor, Red Boucher, both indefatigable campaigners, rolled into high gear. At every opportunity they branded me a "zero growth" advocate determined to lock up Alaska and throw everyone out of work. This played well not only with the Teamsters and other labor unions, but also with the business community. My lead in the polls started to dwindle, then collapsed.

My assertion that some growth and development could be malignant made many restive. Egan and Boucher, sensing a soft underbelly, probed it at every opportunity—sometimes imprudently. Boucher condemned me before the NAACP as a "black-hearted environmentalist," a gaffe that did little to improve Red's ratings in the black community.

Unlike most politicians, who profess to love campaigning, I loathe it. Campaigning should be made illegal. Dashing about, flashing the incisors, and attempting to convince bored, truculent, or uninformed voters that one can best represent them seems not only presumptuous, but a crude attempt to capitalize on the fact most of us are equally ill-informed on both sides of an issue.

The increasing onslaught of political propaganda assailing us from radio and TV does little to upset this balance. Disruption of other programming with campaign blurbs both irritates and fails to impress the electorate. Back in the 1970s few candidates could out-bombast Archie Bunker, though I and many others tried. In an effort to atone, I suggested to my staff that we run a TV ad during the latter days of the campaign that showed a burbling waterfall, instead of a babbling head, introduced by the words: "The following ten seconds of merciful silence are brought to you courtesy of Jay Hammond." I regret we never did so.

Notwithstanding having alienated the largest paper in the state, the National Education Association, the Teamsters, the AFL-CIO, the Republican hierarchy, the Chamber of Commerce, and state employee unions, I failed to lose the election. After three recounts, during each of which my lead was cloven in half, I was finally declared governor by a margin of 287 votes, only three days before having to assume office.

ONE OF THE FIRST OBLIGATIONS of a new administration is to select staff and cabinet. Since my two-year absence from the Legislature and general lack of acquaintance with potential appointees limited my choices, I relied on recommendations from those whose opinions I respected. During my first years as governor I strove to put a balanced team in my cabinet and was therefore berated by both environmentalists and developers for inconsistency and lack of leadership.

This dearth of leadership was evidenced by my inability to curry support for my "Alaska, Inc." proposal, which called for using a portion of our oil wealth to create an investment fund from which dividends would be paid to all Alaskans. In an attempt to gain support for that concept, one of my first acts was to create the Alaska Public Forum. Meeting throughout the state, the forum was designed to showcase Alaska, Inc. and secure enough popular support to induce legislative passage. Alaska, Inc. fell flat. Public response was one massive yawn.

Fortunately, a few visionary legislators such as Oral Freeman, Clark Gruening, Terry Gardiner, Hugh Malone, and Chancy Croft designed a prototype concept that finally flew—only to have me shoot it down in the most painful veto I was ever forced to trigger.

Though these legislators termed it the Alaska Permanent Fund, it was at best semipermanent. Created by statute, it could be invaded at any time by majority vote. To consider it permanent would be akin to deeming the Ten Commandments the Ten Suggestions. Unless it was incorporated into our constitution it would soon disintegrate in efforts to rob it. Accordingly, I vetoed a program that at least took a first step toward accomplishing something I'd worked on for almost fifteen years: translating depletable resource wealth that benefits only a select few into interest-earning assets that would continue in perpetuity and would provide a discernible benefit to every Alaskan.

Hoping yet to accomplish this, I proposed a constitutional amendment establishing the fund and requiring that 50 percent of oil lease revenue, bonuses, royalties, and severance taxes be placed in it, with half of its annual earnings to be disbursed as dividends to Alaskans. In addition, a public vote would be required before one dollar of the fund itself could be spent. The Legislature cut my 50 percent to 25 percent and eliminated severance tax dollars and the dividend—but it passed the proposed constitutional amendment establishing the fund and requiring a vote of the people before it could be invaded. This would go on the general election ballot in 1978. By then I hoped most Alaskans would see the wisdom of doing what I'd termed "translating oil wells temporarily pumping oil into money wells pumping money in perpetuity." They did so and the amendment passed handily.

During most of my tenure as governor, rarely was I prompted to compose the doggerel I used to inflict on my legislative colleagues. For one thing, there seemed little humor in the overwhelming changes taking place in Alaska. During my first years in office, we were required to meet demands of an increasing populace from barely adequate revenues. Later as oil wealth inundated the state's coffers, most politicians could not wait to spend it unwisely.

ONE OF THE MOST LAVISH PROPOSALS advocated construction of several hydroelectric plants. Prime author was Senator Ed Dankworth, an Anchorage Republican. Mercifully, most of Ed's massive hydroelectric projects died aborning. But behind Big Ed's good-ole-boy facade lurked one of the most clever, and perhaps devious, minds to enter Alaska's legislative arena. Ed could charm you out of your socks, and when your toes began to freeze, convince you he'd merely borrowed the socks for mending and that someone else had then stolen them from *him*.

For a few years Dankworth was the Legislature's biggest power broker. Big Ed pulled strings to which more than one political puppet danced. Despite an inclination to hang onto my wallet when in his presence, I rather liked the fellow—at least until I'd read what he had to say about me before the Anchorage Chamber of Commerce. Ed had reinforced his audience's perception of me as a blatant advocate of no growth who would, if not curbed, encompass them within a national park, then tax them as concessionaires.

A bit distraught, I asked why he had blasted me when just a day before he'd been telling me of his high regard and ardent support. Without a shred of shame Ed confessed he was simply playing to his audience. "I admit I'm nothing but a political animal. No one makes points before Anchorage constituents by blessing Hammond; blasting you is what will get one reelected. I readily confess I'm a coward when it comes to politics." Finding his candor refreshing, I restrained the impulse to boot him from my office. Henceforth, however, rather than clutching my wallet in his presence, I made sure I left it home on the dresser before agreeing to an audience.

19 Reluctant reenlistment

Awaiting recount of primary election returns that had placed Wally Hickel ahead, Bella and I contemplate with dismay the possibility of being thrown out of office and into our "briar patch" at Lake Clark. Juneau, 1978

WHILE I HAD NOT PLANNED to run for reelection in 1978, two things compelled me to do it. First was the fact I had not yet fulfilled my intent to guarantee that much of our oil wealth be saved for the future and that all Alaskans receive direct benefits from it. Second, we now had a working administration team for which I had not only admiration but also affection. To not run for a second term would have pulled the rug out from under a lot of fine people who came aboard assuming I'd run again.

Through my first four years as governor, I was jabbed at every turn by former governor Wally Hickel, *Anchorage Times* publisher Bob Atwood, and Teamsters boss Jesse Carr. And I gave them ample targets. Actually, I rather enjoyed jousting with them on occasion. One such opportunity presented itself during the 1978 campaign when I accepted an invitation to speak at the annual Anchorage Chamber of Commerce convention. Upon learning that lunch was being hosted by Hickel, Atwood, and Carr, I had no doubt what was to be featured on the bill of fare: roast bush rat!

Each of my nemeses addressed the group. First was Carr. After cataloging my alleged sins of omission and commission, Jesse launched into a crude ethnic joke, acknowledged the somewhat embarrassed applause, then stepped aside to let Wally take over. After filling in any blanks Jesse might have overlooked, Hickel to the delight of the crowd pronounced that unlike some folks he knew, he was a *practical* environmentalist. Bob Atwood, however, got the most sustained applause in the wake of the following story:

"I UNDERSTAND two environmentalists were out camping one clear, moonlit night. Let's call one the Guv and the other Av (my attorney general was Avrum Gross). While they lay in their sleeping bags staring into the heavens, the Guv wistfully says to Av: 'Gee, that moon must have been pretty once, before they went and walked on it'."

Bob sat down to a standing ovation and everyone commenced eating lunch. I would be allowed to respond during dessert. While pretending to nonchalantly concern myself with nothing more than dismembering my halibut fillet, I was frantically scribbling a response on my napkin. As the gathering attacked their chocolate mousse, I ascended the sacrificial altar.

"Considering what they've read and heard, I don't expect to get the vote of Jesse's Teamsters, though after his comments today I may pick up one or two from those of Polish extraction.

"And so far as Wally Hickel's assertion he's a practical environmentalist, I want you to know I'm a practical *developer*. A practical developer, of course, is one who advocates rational resource development with appropriate environmental safeguards."

And regarding Bob Atwood's concerns about my zeal for preserving wilderness, I came up with a bit of verse that concluded with the following lines.

It's true that I decry trespass on some wild and scenic land
But Bob you've missed my message and can't seem to understand

That I'd like to see you on the moon; I wouldn't lock it up.
In fact, if it were possible, I'd help you rocket up!

Along with the usual indignities heaped on a candidate, my 1978 campaign saw a new one. Staff member Bill McConkey had included an added
attraction on invitations to a fund-raising party for my fifty-sixth birthday:
"Here's your chance to *really* put down a politician! The two semifinal win-
ners of our arm wrestling contest will take on the governor."

Though not happy with prospects of public humiliation, I could hardly
renege on what many assumed, erroneously, was my personal challenge.
After upbraiding Bill for putting me on the spot, it was immensely satisfying
to beat him when he emerged as one semifinal winner. Though at thirty
years of age an intimidating six-foot-three and 230 pounds, McConkey was
not in his prime after arm wrestling fighting through a half-dozen prelimi-
nary contests.

My final opponent, a chubby, baby-faced kid of about twenty, appeared to have made entirely too many trips through the Golden Arches. At
five-foot-eight, he must have weighed at least 220. "A piece of cake," I
thought smugly. Then he took off his shirt. Instead of cake, hard tack! The
lad was built like a cement mixer. I clasped as best I could his salami-size
fingers and watched his enormous arm cord up like a python. Though I'm
sure he could have dumped me immediately, he graciously let me struggle
for a full minute before doing so.

Humiliation eased off a bit when I learned the lad had later won the
state arm wrestling championship. Nonetheless, I felt obliged to try to salvage some pride by making an important point in verse regarding my prow-
ess at arm wrestling.

At age fourteen it was often told of myself
I could whip most men twice as old as myself.

And believe it or not, friends, now as a man
I find that, by golly, you know I *still* can.

Election results in 1978 were the reverse of those in 1974. Instead of winning the primary by a substantial margin and then barely surviving the general, I
barely weathered the primary but won the general by a wide margin.

An opponent in *both* was again Wally Hickel. This time he proved far
more formidable. For one thing, absent was much support I'd received from
dissident Democrats and environmentalists in '74. In 1978 they instead
backed their own candidate, Chancy Croft. Several told me they would have

remained in my camp if they thought for a moment Wally would win, but they felt I'd have no difficulty in besting Hickel. I did not share this view. With something like one in every three voters having come to Alaska since '74, the blend of public perception of Mr. Hickel had changed dramatically. Environmentalists among our new populace brought with them the national perception of Wally, which was much different from that of old-time Alaskans.

In 1974 almost every environmentally concerned Alaskan believed Wally to be a blatant developer who, if given the chance, would plasticize and pave over all of Alaska. However, when Hickel as U.S. Secretary of Interior was credited with saving the beaches of Santa Barbara from oil pollution and rescuing the Florida alligator from extinction, he wore a different mantle in the eyes of many voters. Not only was he sometimes labeled "the nation's leading environmentalist," but he also was one who had told off the then widely despised Richard Nixon. In the primary election, I beat Hickel by ninety-eight votes. (Wally later resurfaced in the general election as a write-in candidate.)

During counting of the primary election ballots, Wally's former attorney general, Edgar Paul Boyko, alleged that Hammond forces had stolen the election. Boyko vowed to overturn it in the courts. Prompting Boyko's aggravation, I suspect as much as anything, was the role played in my campaign by my first attorney general, Av Gross. Boyko seemed to sorely resent that while many considered him bright, most considered Gross brilliant. Here was his chance to "put Gross in his place," which presumably Boyko felt was several notches beneath himself. Ever willing to play the legal swashbuckler, Boyko strapped on his guns and confronted Gross in court for a showdown, grandly pronouncing he would handle the case for a token one dollar.

The courts ruled in our behalf, prompting me to thank Edgar Paul Boyko for making Hickel look bad.

> Those supporting Hammond's reelection
> View Edgar Paul with much affection
> For we doubt when all is done and said
> We could have won without you, Ed.
>
> When the courtroom dust had settled
> It seems that Edgar Paul had nettled
> Much of Wally's old support,
> Some of whom were heard to snort:
>
> "Who's this guy Bilko? What's he doing?
> It seems to us he's really screwing
> Up Wally Hickel's public image
> By losing every courtroom scrimmage."

And sure 'nuf when smoke of battle cleared
The Hammond forces loudly cheered
A once-hidden ally now exposed to all:
Our secret weapon, Edgar "Peashooter" Paul.

And Ed, realizing he'd help us kill
Off Wally's threat, sent *us* the bill.
I took a look and did agree
To pay friend Paul's entire fee.

"After all," said I, "Ed's fee is fair
Not padded as some would declare.
I'll *pay* that dollar, not tell him to shove it.
After all, Ed's worth every *penny* of it.

Once the courts had disposed of Boyko's suit, I went on to win the general election by a wide margin. To their much greater credit, Alaskans also voted overwhelmingly to enshrine a permanent fund in our constitution. However, it lacked what I felt to be a necessary protective ingredient: dividends payable annually to every Alaskan.

One of my first acts during my second term was to once again try to incorporate the Alaska, Inc. concept into the now constitutionally established permanent fund. I proposed, in essence, that one share of dividend-earning "stock" be issued to each person for each year he or she had resided in Alaska since statehood. While the Legislature was willing to test-fly my proposal and it was supported by Alaska's Supreme Court, the U.S. Supreme Court shot it down on grounds it constituted unfair discrimination against newcomers. Only after extensive repatching and overhaul was the current dividend program successfully airborne. This program provides that roughly one half the fund's earnings be distributed each year in equal dividends to all Alaskans.

THE PRIMARY ELECTION of 1980 saw the Reagan and Ford factions of the Republican Party engaged in strident combat. Our incumbent congressman from Alaska, Don Young, was a shoo-in for renomination by the party, but there was no such consensus on a presidential candidate. As a Republican governor, I'd been asked to address the party's state convention in Anchorage in an effort to heal the breach. Reaganites sat on one side of the room glaring at the Ford folks on the other. The tension was palpable. "What in the world have I gotten myself into?" thought I, ardently wishing I'd left my Gerald Ford campaign button at home rather than appended to my lapel, where supporters of Ronald Reagan eyed it as nauseously as they would a pustule.

Discarding my prepared remarks, I chose to wing it. Striding purposefully to the podium, I engaged in no pleasantries and got right down to business: "All right!" I announced sternly. "I'm well aware there's dissension in the ranks regarding which candidate we Republicans should support. However, I believe it *imperative* that before we leave this room we all speak with one voice."

My Ford button seemed to pulsate as glaring Reaganites bore-sighted in on it while mumbling and restlessly shifting their chairs. A quick glance at the table where my staff and my wife Bella sat captured a clearly semaphored message: "What in the world is that idiot up to now!"

As I continued to berate the crowd for failing to close ranks, tension grew. Reagan supporters were muttering imprecations. Realizing I'd best conclude before they started hurling ashtrays, I admonished: "Therefore, I must insist that before we leave this room, we unite behind a single candidate and bend every effort to assure his election!"

At this point several outraged Reagan supporters leaped to their feet and surged toward the door. Before a mass exodus could occur I thundered: "Therefore, I *demand* that we rise as one in support of the *only* Republican candidate who can surely prevail against his Democratic challenger come next November: Congressman Don Young!"

Caught in midstride on their way out the door, several Reaganites—all sporting Don Young buttons—stumbled over each other, their curses accompanied by raucous laughter from delighted Ford supporters. The Reagan crowd was not at all amused. Nor was my wife: "Don't you *ever* do anything like that again. I thought you'd taken complete leave of your senses. Now I *know* it."

20 Captain and crew

Not exactly our everyday attire, but Bella and I were gussied up for a White House function. Washington, D.C., 1978

MY SECOND FOUR-YEAR TERM as governor was a piece of cake compared with my first. A bit stale and crumbling perhaps to some, but cake nonetheless. For one thing, since Alaska's constitution prohibits a governor from serving more than two consecutive four-year terms, no longer was I the target of those wishing to replace me. I would be replaced regardless. In addition, I had acquired a remarkably dedicated and smoothly functioning staff and cabinet that made me look good in spite of myself. And I'd learned to do an end run around the more unfriendly media.

Rather than submit myself to editorial board inquisitions, as I had in my first term, I issued press releases confined to subjects I wanted covered. Moreover, by using newly available satellite television to convey my message directly, rather than having it interpreted by others, I was able to tell folks what I was *really* up to and why. This revised approach was the brainchild of a man who came aboard during the early stages of my 1978 campaign and played a crucial rule in my reelection. With but a 42 percent approval rating at that time, it was evident the Hammond image badly needed reconstructive surgery. This odious task fell to the scalpel of remarkably talented PR expert Bob Clarke. Little did I realize at first that PR actually stood for Perfectly Ruthless.

Dr. Clarke attacked his patient with the fervor of a Dr. Frankenstein. Furiously hacking here and splicing there, his scalpel sliced off all sorts of wens and warts. His resculpted image bore little resemblance to that conjured up by some opponents and members of the press. Clarke's major challenge, however, was my retraining. He sternly advised me henceforth to just grunt unintelligibly when asked probing questions and to confine comments on key issues to those we had worked out in advance. The former proved easy; the latter, a bit more challenging. That his strategy paid off is evidenced by polls taken four years later showing my approval rating had doubled.

For all of Clarke's help and brilliance, how could I possibly reward him appropriately? Since I could not, I rewarded him inappropriately. I often balked at his scheduling suggestions before begrudgingly agreeing to, for instance, climb aboard a llama cart in a parade. For subjecting me to such indignities, I sought revenge. One splendid opportunity occurred when we arrived late for a flight from Chicago. I had advised my staff never to have a plane held up to accommodate me, because I can think of nothing less pleasing to passengers than to learn that a delay is due to some blundering politician. Well aware of my likely displeasure, Clarke also knew that our presence in Alaska was imperative and that in this case he had no choice but to ask that the plane await our arrival. As we stumbled down the aisle, with disgruntled passengers' eyeballs probing our backs like blistering laser beams, I turned to Clarke and inquired: "Well, Governor, did you want the aisle or the window?" With the focus now on poor Clarke, I slumped anonymously into my seat as he slunk into his.

One reward in being governor was the privilege to work with such incredibly talented people. While governors may be pleased to take credit for popular accomplishments, truth be told there are a multitude of "little governors" who can do much either *for* or *to* you. Those that do most to form a governor's image are, of course, members of the cabinet and staff. I was especially blessed in having aboard a remarkable group of dedicated people, all of whom could fulfill their duties far more competently than I. Were that realization not humbling enough, the niggling thought often surfaced they could much better do *my* job as well.

Daily contact with my immediate staff brought a familial relationship. This once prompted me to note facetiously: "You guys treat me almost like a father: arrogant, abusive, sassy, and disrespectful." Actually, most were fiercely loyal, accomplished, and protective. I retain immense admiration and affection for all.

Chuck Kleeshulte, at this writing U.S. Senator Frank Murkowski's highly esteemed press secretary, had been a reporter for the *Juneau Empire* before joining my staff. His reputation for integrity, outstanding writing skills, and encyclopedic knowledge was well warranted. However, soon shattered was his naive assumption that all members of the media were more concerned with "telling it like it is" than telling it as they would like it. He initially felt all I had to do was bare my soul to the media and they would realize what I splendid fellow I *really* was. It was not long before he came to recognize why those in political office become paranoid and evasive. Kleeshulte's belief in media impartiality took an especially bad fall after he read one account of a press conference he had addressed.

When Kleeshulte first came here his sins were but few.
Alas! Now he's tarnished and his halo's askew.
Once wide-eyed and cuddly, he chuckled in glee
At the prospects of trying to sanitize me.

"We'll have open government and every day
A press conference at which we will all have our say.
We've nothing to hide, so welcome the press.
Permit them to probe our every inner recess."

But, brother, to hear him of late you would say
That wide-eyed innocent's long gone away.
Now his eyeballs have narrowed and he terms "verbal vomit"
The distortions they make of *his* every press comment.

One of my most popular and competent aides was V. Kent Dawson. At the time a somewhat rotund, balding, and bearded pipe smoker (a vice long since abandoned, along with excess poundage and remnants of hair),

Dawson served my administration exceptionally well in various positions. As much as anybody, he was instrumental in my reelection in 1978, a fact for which I hope most Alaskans have long since forgiven him.

Dawson was immensely helpful in fashioning means to frustrate efforts to squander Alaska's newfound oil fortune. However, one danger facing anyone serving as my executive assistant was burnout. The effort required to fend off sharks while keeping the governor's nose above water, plus keeping one's cool and sense of humor, extracts a price. Part of that price was having to intercept pleas and complaints that otherwise would be dumped on me. Dawson so charmed petitioners that they were unaware of any black thoughts churning behind his friendly countenance.

When he's pummeled on or screamed at
You may have noticed all the while
That old Kent just sits there radiating
A somewhat hirsute, beneficent smile.

And thus he hides the shocking fact
That behind that sunny smile
He ponders rasping your bicuspids
With a coarse-toothed bastard file.

Or how he'd like to handle
Some pesky legislator's gripe
By spindling, then inserting–
Along with glowing dottle from his pipe–

That legislator's bill portfolio,
Including "letters of intent"
And then watch them rocket from his office,
Flames shooting from their vent.

In recognition of Dawson's sacrifices, at his request I moved him to another slot and appointed the superbly efficient Jerry Reinwand as his successor. Reinwand brought enormous energy, loyalty, and intelligence to the job. An intense individual, he was known with somewhat guarded affection as Bruto by staff and myself, all of whom held him in high regard. At the start of one legislative session, I suggested he utilize a contrivance I had secured in hopes of alleviating my neck and back pain. It was called a back swing. By locking your ankles in place, it allows you to tilt backward and hang suspended, upside down. I suggested he climb upon this queer contraption once in a while to get the Legislature's viewpoint.

A retirement dinner provided opportunity to both buff and tarnish the reputation of cabinet member Sterling Gallagher, commissioner of revenue. I was never quite sure whether Sterling's money management proposals were all wise or all wet. So convoluted was his turn of phrase and incomprehensible his theories that in the wake of his presentations, I'd often ask others to explain in simple English what he meant. Almost invariably they were just as baffled. As a result there was some debate as to whether Sterling was a genius or an idiot.

Seeking clarification from Sterling was unthinkable. So cheerfully confident seemed he that I didn't have the heart to disillusion him by displaying my almost total lack of comprehension. Instead I prayed a lot, and was rewarded: Sterling left the state's exchequer far more solvent than he found it. In appreciation of his talents, I delivered the following bit of verse at his retirement dinner.

> Some folks are known for wisdom,
> Some folks are known for wit.
> But with Sterling we were never sure
> If either label fit.
>
> For behind that grin and verbiage
> We suspect there sometimes flitted
> Two Sterlings: one who was half wise
> The other one, half-witted.
>
> The former lad did magic tricks
> Most wondrous to behold,
> Like some medieval alchemist
> Turning garbage into gold.
>
> But the latter lad was just as apt
> To switch pleasure into pain
> When he'd, without half trying,
> Switch gold to garbage once again.
>
> Now Sterling is departing
> His commission and his post
> And I can't as yet begin to tell
> Which Sterling we'll miss most.
>
> So to both your alter egos,
> Just to save ourselves some trouble,
> We'll pay tribute in exactly equal parts
> And for this dinner charge you double!

Another public servant for whom I had great admiration was Gordon Jensen, a commercial fisherman from Petersburg who sat for more years than anyone in one of the hottest seats in state government: on the Fish and Game Board. Standing over six and a half feet tall and weighing in at 300-

plus pounds, Jensen was a gentle giant whose common sense matched his physical proportions. These qualities earned Jensen sufficient respect from successive governors to assure his retention in a position that too often was used as a political football.

One memorable experience with Jensen occurred long before I was governor, while we were attending a fisheries conference in Tokyo. Jensen and I, along with Clem Tillion and Bob Moss, had summoned a cab. When the driver of the Toyopet minicab opened the door to admit Tillion (195 pounds) and me (210 pounds), he sighed as the springs settled somewhat. When Moss (220 pounds) then climbed aboard, he audibly groaned. However, when Jensen's bulk blocked out the sun and his hamlike fists seemingly spread the door's sideposts to allow his buttocks to enter backward, the driver shook his head and spluttered incomprehensibly as the cab's chassis sank another six inches. The driver's tirade continued until he deposited us at our destination and, still spluttering, drove off in a cab listing badly to starboard. Tillion, who spoke some Japanese, caught but a couple of the cabbie's words—something about whales and sardine cans.

I ALSO HOLD IN FOND MEMORY a number of people who were not part of the administration team, but occasionally seemed almost members of our extended family. There was hyperkinetic activist Dixie Belcher, who was forever embarking on some cause into which she threw not only her abundant energy but also the unsuspecting bodies of those imprudent enough to give her any encouragement. One famous Dixie-sponsored inspiration was the Alaskan Performing Artists For Peace. This group was made up of Eskimo dancers, black gospel singers, and a multitude of other performers whom Dixie enlisted to tour Russia, hoping to spark good will. She insisted that Bella and I accompany them.

This was before the Iron Curtain had been stripped aside, so it took some adroit maneuvering for Dixie to obtain permission to at least peek behind it. But it turned out to be a remarkably successful, if chaotic, tour that included trips into some parts of the Siberian outback long closed to tourists. In "appreciation," I penned:

Through the outback of Siberia,
Our most stark impression was, to whit,
Not of food, language, or the people,
But the toilet paper's grit!

Yet someday when our scars are healed
We'll no doubt all agree
That were it not for Mrs. Belcher
Life would seem entirely too darn free

Of confusion, chaos, panic
And all things which cause dismay
But at the same time increase appreciation
Of the good old USA.

So we love you, Mother Belcher,
Despite some minor faults.
You've richly earned this epitaph,
Well known to old show-business salts:

At your next inspiration, open up your mind,
And hope it will fall through.
But should it not, please remember, Gal,
Don't call us, let us call *you!*

Juneau radio personality Warren Wiley was another memorable individual. Known as Uncle Fats, Wiley was not only an accomplished and prodigious trencherman, but also an ardent and expert fly fisherman. Just prior to my leaving office, Wiley, a Democrat who had worked for the prior administration, came to my office to present a splendid graphite fly rod he had made for me. Though on the verge of retirement, I was reluctant to accept it in light of my directive that members of my administration accept no gifts or services that exceeded $100 in value or could not be consumed within a twenty-four-hour period. However I made Uncle Fats a deal. "You retain the rod until I can compensate you for it by taking you on a fishing trip to Bristol Bay."

A few months later, Wiley joined me at King Salmon—his 250 pounds sheathed in straining neoprene waders, presentation fly rod in one hand, the other clutching his "emergency gear" consisting mainly of martini makings. From there we flew to Brooks River in the Katmai National Monument, famed for brown bears that fish virtually shoulder to shoulder with human anglers. It was not long before Uncle Fats made their intimate acquaintance.

Upon arriving at our fishing hole
Fats grabbed his favorite fishing pole,
Donned waders, tied on "killer" fly.
To believe you'd have to see this guy

Leap into the swift and foaming water,
prepared, I thought, to quickly slaughter
Half the finny, piscatory horde
Until behind him something *roared!*

Next thing I knew that old curmudgeon
was in a state of great high dudgeon.
Seems a bear, a real whopper,
where Fats had been did a belly flopper.

In haste Fats scampered, water flew,
but not before he'd lost a shoe.
But that's not the end of our tall tale.
Seems that as he hobbled down the trail

Fats encountered three more bear,
no farther than from here to there.
This time he shucked both hat and waders.
So clad in naught but soggy gaiters

Wiley scampered back to camp,
grateful no brown bear left its stamp
Upon his desperate, dodging nates
Or propelled him through those pearly gates.

All's well that ends well, so they say.
Yet legend has it to this day
That sometimes on that self-same river
anglers still with laughter quiver

At a one-shoed bear in Wiley's hat.
The waders? Well to answer that,
The reason no bear tried to kill 'im
is there's no bear big enough to fill 'em!

The fun of knowing people like Warren Wiley and Dixie Belcher and hundreds of other fine and fascinating people made my twenty years in public office emotionally rewarding. Greatest of these rewards was the privilege of serving our cherished state for and with a wonderful group of people. Though I miss the fray not at all, I miss this "family" that so enriched my life.

PART THREE

Burning issues still smoldering

21 Ever cry wolf

Warming up to go wolf hunting at 40 below, back when I worked for
the the U.S. Fish and Wildlife Service. Wolves are now highly regarded,
and attempts to control their number meet heated oppositions. Alaska
had far more wolves than people when I came a half-century ago.
Naknek, 1952; James Drew photo

THOUGH MANY ISSUES confronting early Alaska state legisla-tors were at least dampened if not snuffed out, some defied quenching. Instead, gusts from both sides of these controversial matters simply fan flames and continue to blow smoke in the eyes of combatants into the twenty-first century. With often a foot on each side of these conflagrations, not only my *eyes* have been scorched by leaping flames. And no issue burns hotter in Alaska than controversy over wolves.

Alaskans, being Alaskans, have wildly divergent views on a subject that seems to prompt more newsprint and passion than all others com-bined. Want to start a brawl? Question the assertions of someone expounding on wolves—a subject on which almost every Alaskan will claim great ex-pertise. Since truth usually lies lodged between two extremes and does little to pry folks from entrenched opinions, I'll simply cite a few observa-tions made after more than half a century in Alaska as a trapper, govern-ment hunter, game biologist, guide, and longtime resident of a remote wil-derness homestead on Lake Clark where wolves are seen fairly often—five times in one recent month alone. A few years ago a pack of thirty-three wolves patrolled Lake Clark on a fairly regular basis.

Of course the wolf is just what we make it. Vicious vermin? Selective culler of the lame and the sick? Noble embodiment of untrammeled wilder-ness? Trouble is, most folks never get to view wolves save in one dimension, and that mostly from books. Some, privileged to see other facets, appreci-ate the complex character of the wolf. As a result, previous opinions some-times take a 180-degree turn. Such was the case of a young biologist I once worked with who, fresh from the academic ivory tower, quoted Farley Mowat's sympathetic book *Never Cry Wolf* as sacred writ; yet after follow-ing wolf tracks to kill after kill among the then-endangered Alaska Penin-sula caribou herd, he not only tumbled out of that tower but became an ardent advocate of wolf control. The controversy rages hot as ever. Propo-nents of wolf control trot out biologists who support their position; advo-cates of total wolf protection do the same.

Rural subsistence hunters, seeing a decline in local moose popula-tions, indict the wolf. Conversely, animal rights activists, mostly city folk, lay responsibility not on wolves but on natural cycles, deteriorating habi-tat, and bear predation. To bolster that argument, the activists cite studies conducted around the declining Nelchina caribou herd, which concluded that about 90 percent of the moose and caribou kills were attributable to bears, with only a small percentage being wolf kills.

This conclusion contrasts dramatically with that of a study conducted in the same area many years ago by my old cohort, U.S. Fish and Wildlife Agent Bob Burkholder, who probably viewed more wolves than anyone ever has or will again. Burkholder once followed and filmed a pack of six wolves for six weeks. He recorded as wolf kills only those that were easily verified. In an area one hundred miles long by fifty miles wide, thirty-one moose and caribou kills by wolves were located and examined.

Contrary to a presumption that only the lame, sick, and halt are taken, all animals checked were judged to have been in excellent health. No selectivity was noted in age, sex, or condition among the caribou victims. With moose, selectivity was clearly by age: six calves were taken for each adult. The wolves caught their prey by surprise and by the force of their charge. No chase was observed to last more than 350 yards. Even single wolves had no difficulty catching and killing healthy adult caribou. Bear predation was minimal.

The later studies in the Nelchina Basin that found bears to be the prime predator perhaps reflect substantially different circumstances. Without doubt bears are more numerous now than fifty years ago. However, it is also possible many wolf kills were improperly attributed to bears since the latter were found feeding on leavings rather than observed making the kills. Wolves, unlike bears, often leave large portions of prey remains in their wake. Burkholder and I once found twenty-seven reindeer killed in one night by wolves near Pilgrim Mountain east of Nome. The wolves had scissored out a few tongues and prime cuts and left the rest, not to return during the three weeks we monitored the site.

Also contrary to popular belief, a recent news article reported that, according to the Alaska Department of Fish and Game, there have been at least two fatal attacks on humans by wolves in Alaska. In both instances the wolves were thought to be rabid. More recently a six-year-old boy was mauled but not killed by a non-rabid wolf. If prey is depleted, wolves might become desperate, as some folks in the supposedly wolf-infested McGrath area fear after some chained village dogs were killed. However, when local mothers voiced concern that small children might be endangered, they were ridiculed by those who virtually deify the wolf and believe them incapable of such deviant behavior. Perhaps one should keep an open mind.

A recent National Geographic television special told of a remote part of India where several small children had been killed and in part eaten by marauding animals. Since this was not tiger country, most people concluded it to be the work of hyenas or leopards. When a prominent Indian biologist suggested wolves might be the culprit since they, unlike hyenas or leopards, often consume only part of their prey, he was roundly criticized by other equally prominent "experts" who asserted Indian wolves had not been known to attack humans. Only after dozens of attacks and numerous fatalities was it finally discovered that wolves were responsible. So adept had they become at seizing victims that even when families kept children inside, the animals would steal into their huts at night, seize the children, and run off.

Most game managers agree that in certain instances, predator control can be a helpful tool in balancing wildlife populations, but arguments over the methods of control make it difficult to deal intelligently with the subject. Add a heaping helping of politics to this mixture and it becomes explosive. For example, years ago predators were suppressed by aerial shooting, poison, trapping, and bounty payments. Despite these constraints, wolf numbers remained fairly stable. Later, as the pendulum swung from consideration of wolves as merely varmints to wolves as virtual nobility, animal rights activists and an ever-increasing urban population less inclined to hunt or to empathize with those who do were passionately moved to preserve what they thought to be the last of our "vanishing wilderness." The wolf became the prime focus of their crusade. Even though most Alaskan biologists felt some predator control was called for when specific prey populations severely declined, politics compelled them to use the least, rather than the most, surgically selective means.

For example, when the Alaska Game Board in 1978 authorized a modest wolf control program by special-permit aerial hunting in an area where studies showed prey populations had sharply dropped, I was buried under letters of outrage demanding that I, as governor, abort the program. I'm told one letter threatened: "For every wolf you kill, expect to lose one member of your family." Whether by trapping, poison, or aerial hunting, he neglected to say. Having firmly subscribed to the policy of not politically interfering with fish and game management programs advocated by the professionals, I refused. A modest program was undertaken and the moose population increased significantly.

When under a subsequent governor, an even more selective control program was undertaken, an avalanche of opposition persuaded him to overrule the board, for which he was lambasted by the other camp. Opposition to the program was based not so much on the killing of wolves as it was on the means to be used. Rather than allowing nonselective aerial hunting, the program called for wolf packs working in the area of concern to be identified, then shot from helicopters. This was no doubt the most selective means of confining control to just the wolves responsible. However, so outrageously "unsportsmanlike" was the procedure that non-Alaska animal rights advocates proposed a tourist boycott of Alaska unless it ceased. Many Alaskans agreed.

As a result, game managers were directed by the game board to seek other means of control. They decided to use snares instead. While hardly as efficient or selective, for a while the public tolerated this more nearly "out of sight, out of mind" process. That is, until a video recording of some snared wolves was nationally televised, with resultant public outrage. Once more it was back to the drawing board.

Next they tried to address the issue by allowing a "land and shoot" program. This allowed a hunter to spot wolves from the air but required the hunter to land and shoot from no closer than a hundred feet from the animal. Even this offended most Alaskans, who by referendum vote overturned the regulation. When asked for my views on the issue, I said I thought the regulation a bit ridiculous since it was unenforceable. How in the world could a game warden discern, for example, whether the wolf had been shot from the air or the land? Moreover, the hundred-foot distance seemed even more unenforceable. For this reason—and not opposition on my part to wolf control when necessary—I opposed the regulation.

ADVOCATES of limited predator control cite Alaska's constitution to bolster their contention that people have precedence over wolves when populations of prey animals, such as moose and caribou, are insufficient to satisfy hunters of both the human and wolf variety. Our constitution states that "Alaska's resources shall be managed for the maximum benefit of its people." That would seem to shore up the obligation of the state to manage wildlife populations on the basis of "sustained yield," which sometimes requires control of predation. However, opponents of predator control assert that Alaskans who don't hunt should be just as entitled to view wolves. To them this is the "maximum benefit." Of course, the fact is that most people will never see a wolf, even if not one more is shot or trapped. Nonetheless, the *chance* to do so, no matter how remote, means an awful lot to some people. Since I can empathize somewhat with both views, in my eyes the issue is neither black nor stark white, but a disturbing shade of gray.

The irony is that both sides could easily be accommodated without endangering wolves in the slightest. It has been demonstrated time and again that if predators are reduced appropriately, prey species increase and in turn so do predators. Once predators are suppressed and prey species increase, many more wolf pups survive and, like a stretched rubber band, numbers snap back sometimes further than before.

Animal activists cite a balance-of-nature theory that suggests animal populations will find an equilibrium on their own if man stops interfering. Certainly nature's balance has too often been set awry when man jams his heavy thumb on the scale. Should hunters and trappers then be removed from the equation? I don't think so. Eliminate hunting and trapping and you can bet game populations will severely decline, since the people most concerned with their well-being are virtually the only ones paying the price through hunting tags and license fees that help assure healthy habitat and game numbers. Until animal rights advocates are willing to pick up that tab, they should work with, rather than against, those who wish to see our wildlife resources sustained.

Meanwhile, interested parties should read the article in the December 2000 issue of *Audubon* magazine that reveals the startling proliferation of the wolves that were reintroduced into Minnesota. Even wolf lovers are dismayed, yet as in Alaska, few people are willing to accept any means of control, though in the long run such might even be in the *wolf's* best interest.

22 Dividend Delusions

Superior Court Judge Ralph Moody did not look favorably upon my proposal to grant each Alaskan one share of dividend-earning "stock" annually. His ruling was overturned by Alaska's Supreme Court, but the U.S. Supreme Court sided with Moody, for all the wrong reasons.

A FEW YEARS AGO the Princess Tours cruise line gave Bella and me a one-week excursion on a luxurious vessel sailing between Alaska and Vancouver, British Columbia. The company also promoted my book *Tales of Alaska's Bush Rat Governor*. In exchange, it was my privilege to address my fellow passengers on things Alaskan, from controversy over wolves to the state's misunderstood dividend program.

The experience proved enlightening to all parties. To us, the most remarkable thing was that though we normally subscribe to healthy eating, after two days all discipline went to the four winds. For breakfast we ate eggs scrambled, poached, soft-boiled, and Benedict; bacon, ham, and sausage; waffles, toast, and muffins drenched in butter and jam. We assuaged our consciences by also consuming healthy heapings of oatmeal and yogurt. After huge portions of everything that was offered at sumptuous midday and evening meals, no desserts were passed up. The term "low fat" lost all meaning, except that fat would likely lodge *below* the belt. At the end of two weeks, however, to our amazement we had not gained an ounce!

Had salt air, or perhaps a supercharged metabolism kicked into gear by a guilty conscience, expended the calories? Who knows? Certainly the energy required in fulfilling my shipboard obligations did little to burn them. Each day a few hundred of the more than one thousand passengers would gather in an auditorium and subject themselves for about an hour to whatever I wished to lay on them.

My first presentation suggested that few patrons were interested in hearing an old ex-politician expound. Though about three hundred people were seated when I lumbered up to the podium, as I was being introduced virtually three-quarters of my prospective audience rose and left the room. And this was before I'd even opened my mouth! I soon learned that just as I'd reached the podium, someone had spotted a pod of whales in Glacier Bay; my audience had flocked to the foredeck to see the animals. Who could blame them? After all, whale "talk" was likely to be more interesting than anything I'd have to say.

Neither I nor the audience were so fortunate as to have such prime diversion on the second day. The auditorium was packed. This provided a splendid opportunity for me to announce that should they discover anything they liked about Alaska, I would be pleased to take credit. Anything they found less than admirable should be blamed on those scoundrels who followed me into the governor's chair.

I then said that before we got into other subjects, we should briefly examine six beliefs that most people seem to have about Alaska. The interesting fact, I explained, is that the beliefs have one troubling thing in common: they're all wrong. I took the myths one at a time.

MYTH NO. 1: Alaska's Permanent Fund dividend program, which annually sends each Alaskan a check, is socialistic.

FACT: Alaska's unique Permanent Fund program is the ultimate in *capitalism.* In socialism, government takes wealth from the people as it sees fit. By contrast, our dividend program simply gives back to the people a portion of earnings from invested oil wealth that by constitutional mandate essentially belongs to the people.

MYTH NO. 2: Alaska is underpopulated.

FACT: From an economic standpoint, Alaska is overpopulated. In most years we have the highest unemployment rate in the nation. We have far too many people for jobs available.

MYTH NO. 3: Alaska is economically sound because of our vast oil wealth.

FACT: Despite its oil wealth, Alaska is in precarious financial straits and has been termed by some as the "Appalachia of the North." In 2000, Alaska had the second-slowest economic growth of all fifty states. Oil production has declined; our wild salmon fishery has been devastated by cheap farmed salmon from elsewhere; the mining and timber industries are in decline or disarray.

MYTH NO. 4: Alaska wisely eliminated its income tax.

FACT: The move was hardly wise, though wildly popular. Alaska's elimination of its income tax was perhaps the dumbest thing we have ever done. By doing so we embarked on a course of *uneconomic* development that generates less revenue than required to sustain it.

MYTH NO. 5: Alaska's wolves are endangered.

FACT: Wolves endangered? There's little doubt there are far more wolves in Alaska now than when I first came here in the 1940s.

I've already told you perhaps more than you wish to know about wolves in the previous chapter. However Alaska's confusing economic situation and its annual dividend payment for state residents warrants further discussion.

When Alaska oil began flowing, the state was engulfed in billions of dollars from oil taxes and sale of oil leases. Since oil is a finite resource, a few of us thought it prudent to invest the bonanza and spend only some of its earnings for government—instead of spending those non-recurrent dollars on recurrent government programs such as education, health and welfare, and police protection. My chief reason in running for governor was to pursue that objective.

Resource rip-offs in Alaska and elsewhere had demonstrated the imprudence of assuming that ephemeral resource wealth would sustain a healthy economy. Many Alaska fishing villages, for example, though blessed with an incredibly valuable resource—their fish—had little to show for its extraction but rural slums. Most profits went elsewhere. Profits remaining were often rashly spent on programs that could no longer be funded in poor fishing years.

I hoped to prevent the same mistake with our oil wealth. Accordingly I proposed the state create a conservatively managed investment account into which half our oil wealth would be placed. To protect the fund from invasion by politicians upon first provocation, I demanded it be enshrined in our constitution and that a public vote be required before its corpus could be invaded. To further bolster protection and gain public support, a distribution of annual dividends was proposed.

My desire was to issue one share of dividend-earning stock in what I called Alaska, Inc. to each person for each year of residency since statehood in 1959. Unfortunately, not only did the "share per year" concept fail, but also my suggestion that application for one's annual dividend be made when one voted fell on deaf ears. Too bad. Children under eighteen of course could not vote, hence their shares would have gone into trusts to be redeemed only if and when they commenced voting. The dollars by then accumulated would provide a fine launching pad either for entering college or the workforce. I suspect such requirement might also have done much to overcome voter apathy. Instead of our usual less than 40 percent participation, we'd likely astound the nation with a 110 percent turnout!

Only after much cajoling, compromise, prayer, and downright blackmail did something resembling Alaska, Inc. and a dividend program pass the Legislature. Before legislators quartered my proposed contributions to the Permanent Fund, I had envisioned using half its earnings for dividends and the other half for government programs. However, when along with those reduced contributions our state income tax was repealed, I feared the only way to have dividends of sufficient size and to prevent them from being eliminated by those wishing to use the money to supplant the lost income tax dollars was to make them the sole priority. Though to its credit the legislature subsequently deposited billions of dollars into the fund in excess of that required by law, the enlarged dividends have retained that protected status.

Meanwhile, loss of income tax dollars and declining oil revenues have caused the Legislature to cut government programs dramatically in an unsuccessful effort to fill a widening budget gap between recurrent revenues and recurrent expenses. For the past few years that gap has averaged about $500 million annually. Declined budget reserves have been used as backfill. Recognizing that these will likely run out by 2004, in 1999 the governor and Legislature proposed new "revenue enhancements," which included dipping into earnings of the Permanent Fund. While they could have passed these without a public referendum, they prudently chose to place their proposal before the electorate. Eighty-three percent voted against it. Obviously the dividend program has done its job—too well, in the eyes of politicians who would love to get their hands on those earnings.

And what was the dividends' job? My candid answer was simply: "to counter *selective* greed with *collective* greed." Prior to the program of annual dividends to every resident, much wealth acquired by government went out in what I termed "hidden dividends" to a select few who knew how to play the game. For example, a year or so prior to the first dividend, loan subsidies not based on need cost the state more dollars in lost potential Permanent Fund interest than did our first year's entire dividend dispersal of one thousand dollars per resident. Yet the former went to less than 9 percent of Alaskans while the latter was equitably dispersed to 100 percent.

The dividend program has more than met its objective in creating a militant ring of defenders who threaten to slaughter any politician imprudent enough to suggest spending Permanent Fund earnings that might otherwise be used for dividends, though nothing in current law prevents legislators from so doing. Fear of voter retribution, the unwise elimination of our state income tax, and sensitivity to voter complaints of excessive state spending have stretched the Legislature on a rack of its own making. Some people believe dividends should either be reduced or capped before new taxes are imposed or government programs are cut. I vehemently disagree. If new revenues are required, either programs should be cut or new "revenue enhancements" imposed that will claw in whatever money is necessary. Dividends provide Alaskans with at least a little assurance those claws won't sink too deep.

I make no apology for believing dividend dollars should *never* be used to supplant tax dollars for funding government. The use of tax dollars makes far more economic and social sense. If we raid prospective dividend funds, each such dollar used for government spending costs *all* Alaskans 100 cents. But by using taxation, at least thirty cents of each tax dollar could be gleaned from Alaska's transient seasonal workforce and burgeoning tourist industry. The remaining seventy cents would be paid by those of us in Alaska who can best afford it.

Unfair to workers from elsewhere? Not really. Since most come from states that impose income taxes on earnings transients make in Alaska, all we'd be doing is transferring those tax dollars from their home states to

Alaska, and that fails to curdle my conscience. After years of witnessing, for example, almost 65 percent of Alaska's fishery payroll leave in the pockets of nonresidents while Alaskans pay the tab for fishery management, protection, and rehabilitation, I think it high time outsiders pay a bit more for the price of admission.

The use of Permanent Fund earnings for government spending instead of for dividends has precisely the same effect as levying a head tax on every Alaskan while leaving transient workers completely untaxed. Destitute Alaskans, the working welfare mother, children, and the multimillionaire would all "pay" precisely the same.

AFTER ALMOST TWENTY YEARS, in 1999 Alaska's unique dividend program suddenly gained worldwide attention. First I received a call from Danish broadcasters asking if I would submit to a TV interview on the subject. They explained that resource development in Greenland had benefited only a few; many Greenlanders felt themselves worse off than before. Next, a group in British Columbia called, asserting that an Alaska-style dividend program should be instituted there for similar reasons. A call then came from the World Bank, inviting me to address its members on the subject. Finally, a group called the Corporation for Enterprise Development wrote to me of their efforts to establish a national dividend program. Their premise was that all citizens own a piece of the sky and should be compensated by those who pollute it. They proposed capping carbon dioxide emissions at the 1990 level and creating a Sky Trust. Rights to pollute beneath that level would be bid upon and a portion of the proceeds dispersed in dividends to all citizen owners. Pie in the sky? Perhaps, but provocative.

Each of these entities felt that of all nations and states experiencing oil wealth windfalls, Alaska had done the best job of management. Norway, which in part patterned its program after Alaska's, was deemed second. All attributed Alaska's success in largest measure to our dividend program.

That's not to say Alaskans are without sin when it comes to wealth management, prime examples being our imprudent elimination of the income tax and our fear of imposing new taxes. Without appropriate taxes, new development with its inevitable population increases does not pay its own way, since the added recurrent expenses of expanding programs such as education cost Alaskans far more than any new recurrent income that is generated.

Unless we cease our promotion of *uneconomic* development, our public sector (government) economy would be far better off were our population halved. Conversely of course, the private sector economy believes it's in Fat City and wants more people, since all those new bodies buy food, cars, and services. Rather than these two economies waxing and waning in concert as they must do almost everywhere else, in Alaska—because we lack appropriate recurrent taxes—when one rises the other falls. These two economies need to be in balance for healthy growth.

Absent recurrent income from taxes, 85 percent of state government funding falls on nonrecurrent oil revenue, which is the same in total dollars whether we have 600,000 residents or 6 million. Use of dividends to fund government would but increase that dangerous dependence.

Without oil dividends for each resident, we would have witnessed the same "business as usual" that has infected other states and nations soaked in ephemeral oil wealth. Special interests who know how to play the game would have ripped off huge "hidden dividends" while the little guy tried to figure out why the blessings of oil seemed to be passing him by. To prevent this, the pitting of collective greed against selective greed has worked beautifully.

28 The great lands of alaska

The Carters visited us at Lake Clark in the summer of 2000. I'm posing with Rosalynn Carter while Jimmy grins with Bella.

UPON THE TWENTIETH ANNIVERSARY of the landmark Alaska National Interest Land Conservation Act—which placed 104 million acres of Alaska's land in parks, monuments, and refuges—I was invited to a roundtable discussion with former president Jimmy Carter and his former Secretary of Interior, Cecil Andrus. Both had presided over passage of the measure in 1980. Though deplored by many Alaskans at the time as a federal land lockup that would cripple the ability of the state to sustain itself economically, time has blunted the aggravation of many people and muted the predictions of doomsayers.

The reception accorded Carter and Andrus back in the 1980s when they visited Alaska stood in stark contrast to that experienced during their anniversary visit in 2000. This time they received more accolades than acrimony. Mo Udall, who as a congressman from Arizona had been a prime legislative architect of the Alaska National Interest Land Conservation Act (ANILCA), noticed a similar change in attitude when he returned to Alaska several years after its passage. "My, what a refreshing change," he said. "On this trip when people wave at me they do so generously with all five fingers."

Carter and Andrus received a warm welcome not only from the faithful cadre of conservationists who attended each gathering, but also from several people who had at first vigorously opposed the measure. Particularly notable were some business folk from Seward who had feared the "lockup" would destroy their community. Instead, a burgeoning tourist industry has arisen largely because of the protected status accorded the Kenai Fjords, now a prime attraction that draws thousands of people to Seward each year. Certainly few can dispute that most folks who visit Alaska do so not to observe clear-cuts or strip mining, but for a glimpse of Alaska's abundant wonders in a pristine state.

That's not to say the Carter and Andrus visit was without critics. Alaska governor Tony Knowles issued a scathing rebuke to Carter for having "used your visit to petition President Clinton to arbitrarily invoke his powers under the Antiquities Act to change the current status of the Arctic Wildlife Refuge to that of a national monument, thereby precluding the possibility of oil exploration." Since a majority of Alaskans favor oil development in the Arctic National Wildlife Refuge, the governor's diatribe no doubt played well in many quarters. However, some deemed it mean-spirited and certainly at odds with the position endorsed by the governor's own Democratic Party when it went on record as opposing oil development in the refuge (usually referred to as ANWR, and pronounced AN-whar).

Clinton did not declare ANWR a monument, believing opposition in Congress to oil development sufficient to provide protection. The administration of President George W. Bush, on the other hand, advocates oil development in ANWR, and congressional opposition appeared to be waning.

While governor I was concerned that oil exploration in the huge refuge in northeastern Alaska would do violence to natural values such as the Porcupine caribou herd that calves on the arctic plain. At the same time, I believed that under certain conditions, limited oil exploration might be acceptable. As part of a proposal for incorporation into ANILCA, I included the possibility of exploration in the refuge in exchange for a ban on oil leasing in Bristol Bay, a far more environmentally sensitive area through which the largest red salmon runs in the world migrate and where an incredible variety of sea mammals and bird life is found.

That proposal would have managed entire ecosystems in such a way as to permit rational resource development while providing environmental safeguards to protect natural values such as migrating caribou and spawning salmon. These creatures of course do not confine their meanderings to areas in which they receive adequate protection, such as a park or refuge. They migrate through adjacent lands owned by the state, federal government, Native corporations, and private parties where the degree of desecration allowed is often left to the whim of the landowner. How much better I felt it would be to evolve a plan that assured adequate protection over the entire ecosystem rather than, say, creating a park where there might be 100 percent protection only to have it abut lands where the owner would subordinate protection to economic development.

My cooperative ecosystem management proposal received encouragement from several congressmen, including Mo Udall and John Seiberling, both prime proponents of protecting Alaska's wilderness. "Makes sense," they told me. "But can you sell it to conservationists?" I could not. While many in Alaska understood my objective, most non-Alaska conservation groups were bore-sighted in on specific areas that in their view had to be declared completely off limits. In these they opposed any development whatsoever, even if it would do little or no violence to the land or its creatures. Ignored was the opportunity to upgrade habitat protection over the entire ecosystem in exchange for permitting only compatible development.

I find it ironic that some powerful national conservation groups now advocate ecosystem management. Because of their opposition at a time when it might have flown, I fear it is now too late. Commendably some organizations such as the Nature Conservancy and the National Park Service are now buying some private lands adjacent to protected areas.

WHEN I RETIRED from public office, I accepted a seat on the board of the National Audubon Society. I hoped I could persuade that organization to help provide the protection I felt necessary for some of Alaska's prime natural areas without precluding rational and environmentally sensitive resource development. Therefore when the issue of whether to open the Arctic National Wildlife Refuge to oil exploration became a national debate, I argued for a somewhat different position than that taken by other conservation organizations such as the Sierra Club and Wilderness Society, which had issued a simplistic "No!"

With the help of fellow member Scott Reed, an exceptionally wise and personable attorney with a kindred warped sense of humor, we drafted a resolution that could be interpreted as either a conditional "Yes" or a conditional "No." Stipulated were conditions that if met would elicit support of Audubon for oil exploration in ANWR. While each condition on its own merits made sense and could hardly be argued against, the likelihood of all being complied with was small. The resolution passed unanimously and I was able to return home to Alaska and retain my scalp, something I could never have done had I been associated with an unequivocally negative Audubon position.

While the resolution was the essence of reason, you may have noticed reason does not always prevail when it comes to political decisions. When two members of the national Audubon Board who represented oil interests returned to their corporate board rooms, they were castigated for what their CEOs concluded was but another impediment to opening ANWR. At our next meeting these penitent gentlemen attempted to overturn our original resolution. However, when we again went through the resolution, propriety prevailed over penance, for there was simply no argument against the desirability of each stipulation.

Among those stipulations was a verification by an entity such as the National Science Foundation of claims that ANWR development was crucial to our nation's energy needs; a conclusion by Congress that such development would not drastically harm the Porcupine caribou herd; and a prohibition of such activities until there was in place a comprehensive national energy policy that emphasized conservation. All board members, including our two oil men, again approved the resolution.

In the wake of this action, Audubon lobbyist Liz Reisbeck contacted me. "I was impressed with your arguments supporting Audubon's position," she told me, "and would like to present them in a letter to every member of Congress. Would you write them up?"

I talked Liz into drafting a letter with my arguments. Her draft letter was a pretty good synopsis, so with some minor amendments I signed it and sent it back to her. A few weeks later I was forced to try to recall just what my letter said when I received a note from Congressman Mo Udall that read: "Right on as always. I couldn't agree more."

"Oh, oh," I thought, "that letter is liable to cause repercussions." At that time Mo was being demonized in Alaska as one bent on stifling economic development in favor of environmental preservation, and I feared his support would earn me horns and hoofs to go along with the forked tail already appended by most developers. That fear was compounded when, shortly thereafter, I received a note from Sierra Club president emeritus Ed Wayburn: "Just saw your letter to Congressman Don Young in the *San Francisco Chronicle*. I thought it was wonderful!"

To my great surprise neither the *Anchorage Times* nor our congressional delegation, all of whom ardently supported ANWR development, issued a word of condemnation. Could it be I had succeeded in confusing everybody?

In Alaska, where a politician is required to dance with alacrity between warring factions, I'd concluded that the best one could hope for was to alienate both sides equally—or completely confuse them. I apparently achieved the latter in this instance. I reached that conclusion when a conservationist ardently thanked me for opposing ANWR development while someone else thanked me profusely for supporting it. I confess I did not try to enlighten either.

THERE HAS BEEN a lot of bombast from both advocates and opponents of oil development in the Arctic National Wildlife Refuge. As usual the truth lies somewhere between the two extremes. For example, I cannot buy the assertions of those who contend oil exploration could not take place in ANWR without devastating the Porcupine caribou herd. As a biologist with the U.S. Fish and Wildlife Service back in the late 1940s, I participated in the first comprehensive survey of the Porcupine caribou, and later I observed the relatively benign environmental impact of oil exploration on the Alaska Peninsula and in Prudhoe Bay. Thus I cannot with intellectual honesty assert that oil activities could not be conducted without excessive environmental desecration.

On the other hand, those who contend that ANWR's potential oil reserves are crucial to our national energy needs or will serve to wean us from dependency upon foreign supplies are equally deluded. Moreover, does it really make a great deal of sense to deplete our own oil reserves at a time when foreign oil is readily available? I would much prefer that we import all that we can and stockpile it while we can—withholdinng our own for a time when foreign oil may not be so available.

As mentioned previously, I tried as governor to use ANWR somewhat as a bargaining chip in securing greater protection for the more-fragile Bristol Bay. At that time I was, I believe, the only public official in Alaska who opposed offshore oil development in the bay. Every previous governor had supported it, our congressional delegation did so, and even local Native corporations were in favor. Subsequently all have gotten religion and turned 180 degrees. Even our congressman, Don Young, hardly known for his environmental extremism, has suggested we buy back any oil leases that may have been issued in the area. So the Bristol Bay issue has been resolved. However I think we should still use ANWR as a bargaining chip by denying entry into ANWR at least until such time as we have in place a comprehensive national energy policy that stresses conservation to a far greater degree.

So I must confess to mixed feelings in regard to ANWR. As one who came to Alaska in 1946 when the population was but seventy-two thousand and found it a bit crowded even then, I admit that from a selfish standpoint I much preferred the backcountry of Alaska before it was invaded by oil development. On the other hand, there's no question about it: oil has contributed tremendously to our economy.

JIMMY CARTER was both criticized and commended during his visit to Alaska in August 2000 when he reasserted his belief that the Arctic National Wildlife Refuge should be off-limits to oil development. The ensuing barrage of editorials and letters suggested as much commendation as condemnation. To my surprise, a recent poll claimed that a relatively high proportion of Alaskans—about 40 percent—now are opposed to invasion of ANWR for oil development.

Certainly Carter's visit played to a mixed audience. Environmentalists seemed intent upon beatification, while Governor Tony Knowles, along with ardent pro-developers and their trumpet, *The Voice of the Times,* cannonaded him. Though acknowledging Carter "may be a nice man," though deluded, the *Voice* derided his "lackluster presidency."

While I once shared that view, time's passage compels reassessment. Certainly Carter's conduct in office lacked the "lust" that comprised much of the luster emanating from, say, Jack Kennedy or Bill Clinton. Titillation reflected from the sordid actions of those more colorful and charismatic rogues casts a far ruddier glow than that from the steadfast fidelity of a Sunday School teacher whose greatest sin perhaps was in perusing *Playboy.*

We empathize with and perhaps admire more those public figures who spice up their terms with lurid peccadilloes than those whose personal lives are less prurient. That they can engage in more flamboyant indiscretions than perhaps we do, and get away with it, seems to salve the conscience and render our own frailties less consequential. Conversely, conduct more impeccable than our own leaves us discomfited and labels the practitioner "pious"—that most damaging of political accusations. We don't like people so much for what they are as for what they make us think of ourselves. Hence when we compare perception of our own morality with that of Nixon, Kennedy, or Clinton, few of us come up wanting.

In the short term we may find color and charisma more impressive than character and accomplishment, but with time's passage, history casts a brighter glow on the latter. Harry Truman, for example, who was once derogatorily referred to as the little haberdasher, was at first considered leaden and uncharismatic. But through time's slow electrolysis, that lead has been replaced in the public mind with the hardened blue steel of his character.

So it may be with Carter. While most agree he might be our greatest *ex-president* for his continued global peace efforts and his concern for the disadvantaged as evidenced by pummeling nails for Habitat for Humanity, they consider his presidency second-rate. I once agreed, but now find it increasingly difficult to determine who he is second-rate to.

The measure of a public figure's stature and legacy should be content of character and significance of accomplishment. By those standards Carter has to be ranked far higher than he has been to date. Oddly enough, that anti-Carter editorial in the *Voice of the Times* compelled me to reach that conclusion. The editorial stated: "Surely you remember the hallmarks of Carter's failed presidency? Skyrocketing inflation that crippled the economy. Rising energy costs. Iran hostages. Soviet invasion of Afghanistan. The Panama Canal giveaway. The Mariel boatlift. More than 150 million acres of Alaska locked up forever."

Hey, wait a minute, isn't it a bit inconsistent now to deny, as did the *Voice*, Bill Clinton any credit for our booming economy, asserting that factors beyond presidential control play the key role, and then blame Carter for sending the economy into a tailspin? Can't have it both way, guys. Moreover, forces beyond Carter's control brought high oil prices, the invasion of Afghanistan, and the taking of hostages. And did Jimmy *really* pipe aboard the Mariel boat people, as some would have us believe? Certainly he can be largely blamed for passage of the Alaska National Interest Land Conservation Act (ANILCA) and approval of the Panama Canal transfer by acts of Congress—but for the former he appears more blessed than blasted by most Americans. Even transfer of the canal, though still controversial, is now widely viewed as an act of courage exceeding that displayed by four of his predecessors, all of whom promised that transfer but then buckled under political pressure. Whether a wise act or witless I can't say, but hardly lackluster.

As a Republican I never thought I'd be defending a Democrat. But contrasting his record to those of other presidents often held in higher esteem suggests we are more conned by style than substance. Consider: what leaps into mind when one thinks of Kennedy? Vietnam, the Cuban missile crisis, the Bay of Pigs, Camelot, and Marilyn Monroe. Lyndon Johnson? Body bags, the less-than Great Society, and his flaunted, flaccid scarred belly. Richard Nixon? Improved diplomatic relations with China, wage-price controls, and Watergate. Gerald Ford? A caretaker presidency and the pardon of Nixon. Ronald Reagan? Massive tax cuts coupled with a huge deficit. George Bush? The Gulf War and "Read my lips." And Bill Clinton? Well, enough said. Talk about a mixed, rather odoriferous bag!

By comparison, credit (or condemn) Carter for at least four monumental accomplishments: the Camp David peace accords between Israel and Egypt; ANILCA, deemed by conservation organizations "the most significant environmental legislation in history"; the Panama Canal transfer; and negotiation of the release of the American hostages in Iran, for which he received almost no credit because the release was calculatedly not implemented until he left office.

Most important, however, Carter, though a Democrat, is a pretty good fly fisherman. Moreover, he has retained his sense of humor. When he and wife Rosalynn visited Bella and I at Lake Clark, I asked if he still had the riding crop I presented to him in 1978. He assured me he did. That presentation was occasioned by something Carter said in the confines of the Oval Office when a staff member asked him what he would do if Teddy Kennedy ran against him in the presidential primary. His response, "I'll whip his ass," was reported in the nation's papers the next day and brought a collective gasp from many who expressed shock that Sunday School teacher Carter would use such an earthy expression.

Shortly thereafter, while attending a reception for Carter, I tried to bail him out by putting a proper spin on his comment "The president," I said in giving him the riding crop, "was of course using the term in the biblical sense and referring to the symbol of the Democratic Party, though most members thereof I suspect prefer the term donkey. As a Republican, I wish to commend him for his candor and encourage symbolical flogging of all who ride to the polls astride that beast. Accordingly, here is an item which should facilitate that. I urge you to apply it unsparingly to Teddy's hindquarters during the primary and, should you win, use it in *self*-flagellation come the next general election."

Along with the riding crop I offered the following:

Said the elephant to the Democrat's steed
"How could it have come to pass?
Your party chose, not a grand mascot like *me,*
But rather a loud, braying ass?"

Said the ass to the pachyderm: "Just look at you.
When they fashioned you someone was drunk.
And to mark your brain end they were forced to append
That ridiculous thing called a trunk."

But on one issue they're in sad accord,
Be they elephants or stubborn mules:
Both are forced to agree neither party has
The market yet cornered on fools.

24 More knots to untangle

My advocacy of studying an alternative oil pipeline route was one of the issues that almost tripped me up. The issues of subsistence hunting and the power of legislative chairmen also kept me hopping.

WHETHER WHILE GOVERNOR or as Joe Citizen, it seems like the same old issues keep nagging at the state. But if I were a dictator, I know how I'd try to resolve two of the more persistent: the subsistence hunting issue and the arbitrary powers of legislative committee chairmen.

More than two decades have passed since Congress required Alaska, if it was to retain management of fish and game on federal lands, to provide a priority for rural people when those resources were inadequate to accommodate all prospective users. Congressional intent was to assure that Alaska Natives could continue to hunt and fish for subsistence use as they had traditionally—even on newly designated parklands, where such activities are normally prohibited. But since most members of Congress opposed discrimination by race, they took a back-door approach to accommodating Native people: priority was granted rural residents, 90 percent of whom are ethnic Natives.

Many Alaskans felt Congress had no business attempting to dictate who can hunt and who can fish based on residency, whether urban or rural. Virtually all Alaskans support subsistence use as a top priority during a time of shortage of fish or game. However, when Congress granted rural users first crack, many nonrural people, who felt equally or more dependent upon those resources than some rural folks, were outraged. Congress created a ridiculous situation where a millionaire who lived in a rural area might be allowed to "subsistence-hunt" on national park lands while a destitute urban Native who had subsisted off those lands most of his life could not.

My preference was to accommodate subsistence needs through flexible regulations rather than inflexible law. I believed that we could designate methods, means, seasons, and bag limits in a way that all Alaskans—urban and rural, Native and non-Native—could be treated equally while requirements for true subsistence needs could be adequately protected.

Instead, Alaskans some twenty years ago approved by public vote a rural preference that appeared to meet the congressional mandate. A dissident urbanite sued, however, and the State Supreme Court ruled a preference based solely on residency violates Alaska's constitution. Absent a state provision of rural priority, the federal government finally, in October 1999, took over management of fish and game on federal lands and certain waters of Alaska.

Alaskans have not yet felt the full implications of the federal takeover, but a congressional mandate that subsistence fishing be granted highest priority alarms commercial fishermen. Presumably the feds could demand sufficient salmon arrive upstream to satisfy rural villagers' needs before downstream commercial fishing could begin. Of course, by then it would be too late since most of the run would already have passed through the commercial fishery.

With the situation still unsettled, there seems to be growing concern among some Alaskans about what they view as abuse of subsistence privileges. For example, the harvest of beluga whales in Cook Inlet has recently exceeded by far the "customary and traditional" level of historic harvest, placing their declining numbers in jeopardy. Moreover, since an allowance for bartering was written into the federal law, the sale of whale parts and salmon roe has affronted many Alaskans. In 1999, subsistence users in the western Brooks Range said they needed the entire Dall sheep allocation (twenty-two animals) for their own needs, despite the fact that the "customary and traditional" level of subsistence harvest historically had amounted to almost nothing. Even most Natives from urban areas no longer support an exclusive rural priority.

Perhaps the most glaring defect of an exclusive rural preference is illustrated by the fact that if, say, a subsistence-use-only caribou season were invoked on the North Slope, hundreds of miles from my home, I could be entitled, by virtue of my rural residency, to participate while a Barrow-born Eskimo who had recently moved to Fairbanks would not, despite having hunted the North Slope for years. Not only unfair, ridiculous.

I believe there is a simple solution to deal fairly with subsistence hunting and fishing: Pass a state constitutional amendment that *permits* (not mandates) the state to use local residency as *a* (not *the*) criterion for determining eligibility. Then invoke a subsistence-use season *only* when the "customary and traditional" level of harvest cannot be met without further restrictions.

Such an amendment would treat all Alaskans alike and therefore remove a major objection to an amendment that would discriminate between Alaskans. It could also accommodate non-rural Alaskans, including many urban Natives, who might qualify through such criteria as dependence on subsistence hunting or history of past subsistence activities.

For the moment, the subsistence issue has been stuffed back into Pandora's Box. However, the lid will not latch. Feeding on speculation, suspicion, confusion, and animosity, the beast within is alive and kicking. I am convinced the difficult issue of subsistence hunting and fishing could be resolved with minimal pain if we allowed common sense and the public interest to prevail. Too bad that under current political practices it is so hard for this to occur.

PROPOSED LEGISLATIVE ACTIONS having broad public support, such as an Alaska constitutional amendment on subsistence, are often thwarted by a practice that prevents majority rule from prevailing at both state and federal levels. This is the vesting of arbitrary power in committee chairmen, permitting them to lock up legislation they don't favor.

This practice fosters gridlock, voter frustration, and demands for campaign finance reform. It means special interests need only one powerful committee chairman in their hind pockets to control the flow of business.

I had occasion to point this out many years ago when I was asked to speak at a budget conference called by then Governor Walter Hickel. During my presentation I suggested a dozen means by which the state could either cut the budget or increase revenues with little pain. These included such proposals as imposing a fish severance tax, which, like a portion of our oil wealth, would go into the Permanent Fund to be dispersed in benefits for all Alaskans.

At the conclusion of my presentation, Natural Resource Commissioner Glen Olds hurried up, pencil poised, and eagerly asked: "Great ideas! I got seven of them, what were the other five?" As he hastily scribbled them down, a few legislators came up and also enthusiastically expressed support for my proposals: "We're going to do them!"

"No you're not," I responded. "You're not going to do any one of them."

"What do you mean?" was their abashed reply.

"All those proposals have two things in common: put them on the ballot for a public vote and all would pass; subject them to the legislative process and not one will. For example, while there can be no doubt the public would approve receiving a portion of Alaska's fishery wealth, just as they now do from oil, do you think for a moment a committee chairman representing a fishing constituency would permit any such bill referred to his committee to see light of day? Of course not. The same is true for any measure which offends one special interest or another despite the broad public interest being best served." Such proved true. Not one of those twelve proposals has made it out of the Legislature.

Lawmakers have permitted a system to evolve under which arbitrary authority is held by committee chairmen who determine which bills live and which bills die. Chairmen wield this power knowing that members of their majority party will almost never vote to extract a bill from committee over a chairman's protest because of possible retribution when an offended chairman gets one of *their* bills in his clutches! This situation creates gridlock even on matters approved by both the executive branch and the legislative majority.

For example, one Senate Rules chairman, who controls the flow of legislation, once refused to release two crucial measures until passage of a bill that blatantly accommodated one of his clients. Weeks and millions were added to that session's length and cost before that obstreperous chairman released those bills, which had to pass before we could adjourn. This happens time and time again

Only once during my years in politics did a majority member vote with the minority to yank a bill from committee. It happened when I was state Senate majority leader. A committee chairman had promised he would bring a key bill to the floor at a certain time. Until this legislation passed, we could not adjourn. When he broke that promise, the minority moved to have the bill brought to the floor. The majority, including myself, not wishing to offend protocol, reluctantly voted "No."

I advised the recalcitrant chairman, however, that if he did not meet a second deadline, I myself would move to discharge the bill. When he again broke his promise, I made good on my threat and made the discharge motion. The offended chairman called for a party caucus, and we recessed to accommodate him. When he instead fled the building and failed to show up for the caucus, we sent troopers out to retrieve him and then reconvened.

My discharge motion passed despite howls from the chairman and a few cohorts, who threatened to resign. Before they could do so we canned them and appointed a new finance committee. The unbottled measure quickly passed, and two days later we adjourned, no doubt saving the state millions in pork-barrel spending that would otherwise have been required to extract that crucial bill from the chairman's clutches. In the wake of this action, my old cohort Clem Tillion chortled: "Hammond, you ought to get angry more often."

In an effort to put an end to this sort of legislative nonsense, I proposed a rule change that would permit three committee members to call for a discharge vote by secret ballot. This would enable legislators to vote their consciences rather than knuckle under to intimidation. It of course failed. After all, such power is a heady brew savored by committee chairmen from which they'll not be easily weaned. And any effort to change things must have the support of committee chairmen.

A secret ballot discharge procedure could accomplish wonders. No longer could a single legislator frustrate the public interest in behalf of a special interest. Instead, the process would *reverse*: three legislators could frustrate a special interest in behalf of the *public*. With the secret ballot discharge, I suspect we would soon lay to rest the issue of subsistence hunting and fishing and would also find a way to fill the state's budget gap. But until such a democratic process is fostered, expect legislative gridlock and voter frustration to increase.

For now, presumption of "one man, one vote" equity remains a delusion. Unless a constituent is represented by a powerful committee chairman, that constituent is being shortchanged. While the secret ballot discharge would not totally eliminate undue influence accorded special interests, it would at least cost them far more to "buy" a majority vote than just the one vote now required to frustrate that majority. What a refreshing change that would be!

PART FOUR

Didn't you used to
be somebody?

25 Speaking
disengagements

I joined a couple of other ex-governors—Wally Hickel and
Keith Miller—to sign copies of our books for the public.
Anchorage, 2000; Malcolm Roberts photo

EVER SINCE I LEFT public office, I'm often asked: "What are you doing with all that spare time you have in retirement?" My reply: "Still looking for it." Never have I seemed busier. Even the paperwork load is heavier now that I have nobody to fob it off on. Each mail brings requests to look into someone's government glitch, endorse some campaign, speak at a function, or review a book manuscript and write a foreword to it. Responding appropriately would take full time. Instead I've mastered the one-line response, scribbled on the supplicant's letter. Crude, perhaps, but far less time-consuming.

After having written some twelve forewords for books, I've about scraped the bottom of the barrel. My last proves that point. It involves outhouses. Personal experience qualified me to write this foreword to Harry M. Walker's gem of a book, *Outhouses of Alaska,* his pictorial tribute to these bucolic bathrooms.

High time someone enshrined the outhouse in Alaska's archives. Perhaps no institution has contributed more to our democratization and development than this humble structure. Caring nothing for creed, skin color, or social status of those who seek solace within its portals, one moment it accommodates the gnarled nates of a trail-toughened bushrat; the next, with equal magnanimity, the billowing buttocks of one to the manor born.

What other institution would accept without complaint the indignities to which the outhouse is subjected? The Legislature? The courts? The National Organization for Women? Forget it. The outhouse, by contrast, invites abuse, forever turning the other cheek, so to speak. No one is denied access (save during prior occupancy) and never does an outhouse seek revenge upon even its most rank defilers—well, hardly ever.

My Gramma Susie told of when she as a small girl took her pet piglet into a two-hole biffy, only to have the animal dive through the adjacent orifice. There was a happy ending—for the pig. Gramma said little of the heroic efforts required to save the swimming swinelet, but pronounced he was retrieved and lived out his full life span. Seems few aspired to dine on sewage-marinated pork.

The outhouse has at times accorded me refuge for reflection, snow shelter, immense relief—and profound frustration. Like the time I accidentally locked myself in one and was reduced to shamefully hollering for help. (Tunneling to freedom seemed even less attractive. Besides, I had more than enough of that while in public office.)

There's much more I could say about outhouses, but if you've ever used one you've probably already said it—perhaps in the howl of anguish elicited by the mortification of 98.6-degree flesh abutting minus 50-degree plywood. Or possibly an appropriate expletive torn loose upon realization the Sears Roebuck catalog has been stripped of all but its slickest pages?

Of course, like most other institutions, with time's passage even the outhouse has been subjected to character-corroding modifications. These make visitations of yesteryear seem even more heroic. Nowadays, a Styrofoam seat cover may insulate one's nether parts, and a more parsimonious Sears no long supplies free toilet tissue. Instead, most biffies come equipped with rolls of TP, often in effete pastels.

Any wonder we have no more heroes?

AFTER I RETIRED from elective office two decades ago, I felt obliged to accommodate most requests from Alaskans in light of the substantial retirement pay they had provided. The amount was based on a percentage of the governor's current pay, which was far higher than necessary.

In 1978, back when I was governor, the Legislature raised the pay for state legislators—and at the same time boosted the governor's salary to $80,000. I thought the salary obscenely excessive. A proposal to repeal the pay increases had been placed on the ballot, and I urged voters to rise up against those fat salaries. My pious pitch was: "Some ask what I intend to do in retirement. Let me tell you, folks, I won't have to do a darn thing in light of the fat retirement check I'll receive unless you overturn the Legislature's new salary proposal. You ought to do something about that!"

They happily complied, and salaries returned to their prior level—that is, all except those of the governor and lieutenant governor. Unbeknownst to me (honest) was a constitutional prohibition against lowering the governor's salary once it was raised. Talk about feeling sheepish! But no longer. That sheepskin has been shed, along with my sense of obligation to perform at public request for no charge.

This is but one reason I hesitate before accepting speaking requests. Among others is my voice. I'm often asked to narrate public service announcements or speak to some group. Many people say they asked because they are intrigued with the sound of my voice. A newscaster once said he'd "go hear Hammond speak if all he was doing was reading the telephone book." Perhaps *his* intrigue was like that of Gustave Flaubert's in regard to a dancing bear: "It's not that he does it well, but that he can do it at all."

At one time I too was impressed with my voice. That is, until I heard what I *really* sounded like. During college German class, our teacher had a wire recorder into which we practiced our umlauts. On this recorder, my voice sounded like that of the old Lone Ranger: a rich, mellifluous bass. Most impressive. For years I thought that's what other folks heard. Enlightenment came when later I was confined to Bob Jones' cabin at Cold Bay, awaiting evacuation for injuries received in a freak accident. Unbeknownst to the three of us sharing his cabin, Jones recorded our voices on his new state-of-the-art tape recorder, then played it back. Suddenly I heard a rasping voice that sounded like Henery Hawk with a hangover mimicking what I had said. I chided Jones for having such a low-fidelity recorder. Imagine my shock when I heard the recordings of the other guys, and they were right on target. With this shocking revelation I vowed to stifle my speech—a vow Bella asserts I kept for no more than five minutes. Nonetheless, I was sorely chastened. Even today I wince when I hear myself on TV or radio.

I was also reluctant to accept speaking engagements while I was in office because I had no idea whether I'd foul out or hit a home run. Sometimes I'd give a speech that my staff members feared would insult my audience, only to have the talk wildly applauded. Conversely, a speech intended to placate or pander might prompt a barrage of boos. I composed almost all my own speeches and can blame no one else for all the times I marched to my own drummer and fell flat on my face.

A speech-making problem encountered in office continues to plague me in retirement. When I spot someone in the audience who has already heard my material, I seem compelled to discard the prepared speech and fumble my way into uncharted territory. Otherwise I feel like a fraud should I try to fake spontaneity. So inhibiting was this hang-up that I asked staff members who attended one such presentation not to attend the next. Many I'm sure gratefully accepted this directive. Staff members forced to attend by circumstance were instructed not to sit within my vision to my left. Past attendees so seated seemed to aggravate the problem.

Never was this oddball phobia more evident than after a largely ad-libbed speech I gave to the Fairbanks Chamber of Commerce. Since it went over well, I planned not to vary it one iota in speaking the following day to the Anchorage Chamber. I had settled in at the elevated head table at the Anchorage gathering when two elderly ladies scurried up and announced breathlessly: "We just came down from Fairbanks where we heard you speak and thought you were marvelous. We can't wait to hear you again."

Talk about being blown out of the tub! They blew me into the *toilet*. Painfully aware of their presence directly to my left, I tried to avoid glancing at mouths I was sure were gaping in disenchantment as I floundered through efforts to alter my remarks from the previous day so they did not seem contrived. I failed miserably.

I also have to be careful about being presumed to have accepted a speaking engagement without some formal agreement. I adopted this policy when I found to my alarm in May 1998 that I was assumed to have accepted eleven speaking engagements, including four in one day. When I was asked to give a speech, I rarely made an immediate commitment. Instead I advised the requester that if my schedule and weather permitted, I'd consider acceptance. *Consideration* too often got translated as *commitment*. I'd actually made only two such commitments and fulfilled both, apologizing profusely to the other requesters.

Now I send the following form to those requesting my presence:

Being of unsound mind and fading faculties I find it necessary to more formally structure requests for speaking engagements, fund-raising events, or protest marches. In order to avoid embarrassment on my part and outrage on yours, please fill out the following:

Name of Organization:
Subject:
Time:
Place:
Honorarium: _____Yes? _____No? _____Amount
            _____Don't be ridiculous

I sometimes find myself in discomfiting circumstances for which no compensation seems sufficient. Take the time in 1999 I was asked to address the National Association of Newspaper Publishers in Juneau. "I really enjoyed your book," the head of the association said of *Tales of Alaska's Bush Rat Governor*. "Much of what you had to say would not only be enormously enlightening for those who know little about our state, but highly entertaining as well." A sucker for soft-soaping, I agreed to speak, forgetting that soft soap can cause pratfalls.

Just the week before, I'd delivered an informal presentation about Alaska to the board of the National Audubon Society, where my remarks were well-received. I thought a repeat of this talk to the publishers would be a piece of cake. But when I arrived at the engagement, to my consternation there was Governor Tony Knowles. One of my phobias immediately kicked in: he had been at the Audubon speech! Even worse, when I walked up to greet him, I was met with outrage over my opposition to his proposed use of part of the state's Permanent Fund earnings for government spending.

After a heavy dinner, I finally mounted the podium at about 10 p.m. to address my sedated audience. The governor sat glowering in the front row. To compound my problems, I'd not had a decent night's sleep for months and was on a powerful painkiller that had me floating about two feet off the deck.

I wanted to simply state that at that late hour I was not about to subject them to a lengthy oration; I wanted to welcome them, tell a couple of jokes, and then slink away. However, the association's president had specifically asked that I touch on certain subjects. In my stupor I fear that instead I manhandled them. I have no idea what I said, and I'm sure the people who were in the audience don't either. All I recall is that I slogged painfully though a morass of swampy verbiage, leaving muddy footprints on whatever small reputation as a public speaker I might have counter-feited over the years. It was not my finest hour.

Two weeks later brought a happier experience at the microphone. The occasion was the eightieth birthday party roast for Wally Hickel—former governor of Alaska, former U.S. Secretary of the Interior, and one of my principal political adversaries over the years. I began with a few words of apology "to those of you compelled to sit thorough my murky marathon speech to the newspaper publishers last week, with the exception of you, Wally, for when I looked up I saw you mercifully sound asleep." Wally and I had been opponents, but I had come to greatly admire him and felt it time to put our new relationship into perspective.

I started by telling Wally that I wasn't there to jab him. "I'm not going to even warm up the oven, much less try to roast you. After all, I've been doing just that for altogether too many years. Time now to do penance—but not too much. Tonight I want to say a few nice things about Wally Hickel."

With that I explained that while Wally and I had been ardent political opponents, I felt much of that opposition stemmed from the fact we were like two fellows peering at each other through opposite ends of the same telescope, thus getting a distorted view of one another. I had viewed Wally as a wild-eyed developer who if given his druthers would pave over and plasticize the entire state of Alaska, while Wally had perceived me as an irreverent clown determined to lock up the state. Yet subsequently I was to preside over Alaska's greatest period of growth, and Wally was to distinguish himself as a concerned conservationist as Interior Secretary. Moreover, during his second term as governor he gained the respect and admiration of many, including myself, who had previously viewed him with suspicion.

"I regret it took me so long to appreciate the enormous energy, talent, and dedication Wally brought in efforts to improve the condition of Alaskans and Alaska, a state which he clearly loves no less than I. So for any past abuse, injustice, or thoughtless comment I may have inflicted, I want to apologize. You're one hell of a man, Wally Hickel, and for that I wish to salute you. But more importantly, I'm proud to call you my friend."

26 Campaign capers

From the political sidelines I still keep my hand in as a
coach and opinionated citizen. 1998; Joan Ray photo

POLITICAL ENDORSEMENTS from old has-been politicians have about as much substance as chicken lip soup, but a surprising number of candidates have requested I ladle some up. One such endorsement from which a campaign actually appeared to draw nourishment was that of Marco Pignalberi when he ran for the state Legislature against incumbent Ramona Barnes, who had previously won reelection by wide margins.

When Marco's campaign manager called and asked me to serve up an endorsement, I agreed, believing I had nothing to lose. I had frequently crossed swords with Ramona and presumably earned her undying enmity when she suspected I was the cad who once asked an Associated Press reporter: "I wonder what welder does her hair?"

In talking with Marco's campaign manager, I told him: "I don't know what I could say about Marco other than as my administrative assistant he exhibited extraordinary intelligence, total dedication, and absolute integrity. However, in spite of these unique qualities I think he might make a pretty good legislator."

End of discussion. Then came election day, and to the immense surprise of political pundits, Marco won. A few days after the election I flew to Anchorage for some supplies, and a store manager told me: "Boy, you sure made up my mind about this guy Pignalberi."

"What do you mean?" I inquired.

"Why, that campaign ad you cut for him."

"What ad?" I asked.

With that the manager produced a newspaper clipping. Beneath an old picture of Marco and me was the ridiculous comment I'd made over the phone to his campaign manager. To my amazement, three or four other people in the store chimed in to tell me that ad had influenced *their* votes.

Not long after this, while visiting Juneau, a legislator warned me that "Ramona's also in town and says she'd like to see you." Hoping to avoid confrontation, I started to slink out of the capitol building by a rear exit when I noted a figure in white billowing down the hall toward me. "Oh, Governor," she shrilled, "wait a minute." Trapped, I braced myself for being swept off my feet in a cyclonic swirl of outraged indignation.

Instead, I was swept off my feet in an exuberant embrace, accompanied by reassurances that despite our past differences, she knew I really liked her, as evidenced by my support of some legislation she had once introduced. I have come to appreciate and admire many of my old adversaries who were most formidable, and Ramona is no exception. A hardworking and canny legislator, it was not long before Ramona was back in office and Marco was out on his ear because of some indiscretion. Seems my offerings of chicken lip soup are at best but temporarily sustaining, and at worst can cause heartburn.

Two weeks before the August 1986 primary election, I received a remarkable series of four phone calls on the same day. Prompting the calls was a poll indicating Wally Hickel led the Republican field in the gubernatorial primary by a wide margin. The callers? The four candidates challenging Hickel: Joe Hayes, Dick Randolph, Robert Richards, and Arliss Sturgelewski.

Perhaps impressed by the boost Marco Pignalberi was alleged to have gleaned from my endorsement, each caller made a similar pitch: "Look, I'm the only candidate who can beat your old foe Wally Hickel. Right now he's several points out in front, but with your endorsement I believe I can beat him."

I told each one: "OK, here's what I'll do. Whoever the eleventh-and-a-half-hour poll shows to be closest behind Wally is the one I'll endorse in the primary."

"Fair enough. I'll be that candidate," was the common response.

The poll taken just before the primary showed Sturgelewski closest, trailing Hickel by seven points. To fulfill my commitment, I cut a short TV endorsement. After Arliss won a surprise victory in the primary, a reporter asked her on camera: "Just a week ago you were well behind Hickel. To what do you attribute the sudden turnaround?"

"It has to be Hammond's endorsement," she responded.

So Arliss requested a second endorsement, to bolster her chances in the November general election against Democrat Steve Cowper. Meanwhile, however, Sturgelewski made a fatal mistake. She listened to members of the Anchorage business community who advised her to tone down her environmental message. "You're coming across as entirely too green for our comfort," they told her. "To receive our support you should endorse programs such as oil development in Bristol Bay."

Arliss followed this counsel and almost overnight lost the support of environmentalists, commercial fishermen, and Native organizations. When apprised of her stand, I first felt compelled to reject her campaign manager's request that I provide her with an endorsement in the general election. However, after bobbing, weaving, and avoiding phone calls, I received impassioned notes from friends who were her backers and I finally agreed, but only under one condition.

"And what's that?" asked her manager over the phone.

"That you run my comments in their entirety or not at all."

"Agreed. What are they?"

With that assurance I read him the following:

"Many of my fisherfolk friends have asked how I could endorse Arliss over Cowper in light of her support for Bristol Bay oil leasing and his opposition thereto. I agree if that were the only issue it would give me pause. However, I believe that in light of Arliss's impressive legislative record and innate wisdom she will come to realize the hazards of oil development in Bristol Bay and listen to reason. Besides, I must admit to a couple of shameful prejudices I have in regard to Oklahoman Steve Cowper: 1. He sounds kinda funny to an ear tuned to the twang of Vermont, and 2. He's an *attorney*, and most of you know of my low pain threshold for most of that breed."

"And so far as his running mate, the dapper Steve McAlpine, is concerned, I must confess I also have reservations. His sartorial splendor and flourishing follicles trigger both suspicion and envy in an old bearded bush rat not graced with either, and he too is an attorney! Since no attorneys ever seem to agree on which course to take, do we really want to have two of them attempting to steer our ship of state?"

From the other end of the phone line came a few seconds of stunned silence, then a mumbled "Thank you." We hung up.

A few days later Steve Cowper called. "I know what you were up to in the primary, attempting to pick Wally off, but I sure hope you stay out of the general."

"Sorry, Steve, I already offered an endorsement for Arliss in the general, though it's not yet run."

"What did it say?" Cowper asked.

After I'd read it to him, he groaned. "I sure hope they don't run that." Cowper knew of the resentment against the Texans and Oklahomans who competed with Alaskans for pipeline jobs, plus the low regard in which many hold attorneys. "That endorsement could be my coup de grace," he told me.

But my serving of chicken lip soup apparently proved too peppery for Arliss's campaign manager, and it was never used. After Cowper defeated Arliss on election day, she told me of her regret that I'd not endorsed her in the general.

"But I did," was my surprised response. I related the phone conversation I'd had with her campaign manager and told her what my endorsement said.

"Oh no!" she moaned. "He never even told me about it or I'd have had it published full page in every newspaper in the state. I love it."

The subsequent conversation between Arliss and her campaign manager remains mercifully unrecorded.

MANY POLITICAL CAMPAIGNS do little to enlighten the electorate. Controversial issues over which prospective officeholders have little control are given undue focus while less colorful ones over which they *could* exert influence may be ignored. Such was the case during the 1990 gubernatorial campaign. During the primary campaign, TV viewers were obliged each evening to watch two talking heads from opposing parties agonize over how to respond to three questions: "What is your position on abortion?" "Do you favor recriminalization of marijuana?" "What is your view on subsistence?"

While certainly pertinent issues, the likelihood that any candidate would have the slightest influence on how they were resolved was something less than double zero. Marijuana recriminalization was on the ballot to be decided by voters. The Legislature was not about to touch abortion with a *twenty*-foot pole. And after some dozen years of debate, the issue of subsistence hunting and fishing remained unresolved and under litigation; hence the courts, not the candidates, would likely dictate its resolution.

Nonetheless, night after night the assault on our sensibilities continued. Frustrated over constant exposure to telecast inanities while key issues went unexplored, I decided to publicly voice my disgust. I called a press conference, at which appeared several yawning reporters and a couple of cameramen.

First I had to get their attention. A few days earlier, Wally Hickel had announced he would run as a write-in candidate for governor. He stated he'd not planned to do so but was offended when John Sununu called from the White House telling him not to run since Alaska already had in Arliss Sturgelewski a fine Republican candidate. Taking a page from Wally's book, I announced:

"I've called this conference," I intoned solemnly, "to announce my intentions regarding the possibility of entering this year's gubernatorial race as a write-in." Suddenly slumped bodies straightened, cameras focused and pencils poised.

"A lot of folklore recently suggested I might do so," I told the reporters, "but like Wally Hickel, I don't like to be told what to do—so I'm not going to do it." I then went on to explain just what I was really up to.

"Now that I've disposed of one inconsequential matter, I'd like to address three others upon which the media have been wasting a great deal of time. In order to do so I've chosen to write the following open letter to Saddam Hussein." Confusion ratcheted up to total bewilderment as reporters tried to figure what the leader of Iraq had to do with all this. I read the letter to them.

Dear Saddam:

Since your actions may well have greater impact on the future of our state than will those taken by any of our current crop of candidates for governor, we think it equally pertinent to demand of you *your* response to three crucial questions asked each of *them*: What is your position on marijuana recriminalization? Abortion? And subsistence? Be assured we will grant you the same thirty seconds of free media time to respond as has been accorded all other candidates.

To the reporters, I expressed regret the media had wasted so much time trying to catch candidates with their verbal trousers half-masted astride painful issues over which they would have little control, while shortchanging issues over which they could exert influence. "For example," I told them, "I'd like to know what a candidate might try to do to protect or enhance the Permanent Fund and its dividend program."

So far the only candidate who had expressed himself on that issue was Democrat Tony Knowles. Arliss Sturgelewski and Wally Hickel had not. "Come on, Arliss and Wally," I said, "get cracking. So far, a Democrat seems way out in front."

My intent was to get Hickel, who had previously opposed the program of annual dividends to every Alaskan, to at least get on the same track as Knowles on a matter certain to grab the public's attention. Sure enough, a full-page newspaper ad later appeared, indicating Wally would run apace with Tony on that particular issue. He would not permit Permanent Fund earnings to be used for other than dividends or reinvestment.

Message conveyed and mission accomplished, or so I thought. However, at least one reporter remained confused, as evidenced by her asking in dead earnest: "Did you ever send your letter to Saddam?"

Later rumor had it that Hickel, who was soon back into the governor's chair, was about to approve use of Permanent Fund earnings for some other purpose. This prompted me to fly to his defense in an article asserting such scurrilous rumor must be untrue in light of the full-page ad, which I included, along with my indignant assurance that Wally was an honorable man who would never renege on that promise. And he never did.

27 Rough running

If down the primrose path of politics
I ever again should travel
I'll take a bigger veto ave
And more persuasive gavel!

WHILE AN IMMENSE PRIVILEGE to serve as governor, it was not always a great pleasure. As I completed eight years in office, a questioner wondered if I could run again. My response: "I'm prevented from doing so by both constitutional constraints and common sense."

However, our state constitution does not prevent a two-term governor from running again after an intervening term held by another governor. Hence, when four years later a reporter asked: "Are there any conceivable circumstances under which you might run again?" I could not cite legal constraints as an excuse for not doing so. Neither did I wish to confess that I questioned my dedication to public service since it now felt so good to not be rendering any. Fumbling around for an answer, I responded hesitantly: "Well, I suppose so."

Interest piqued, he pulled out pad and pen, asking: "And just what might those be?"

"First, Wally Hickel would have to agree to run as my lieutenant governor," I told him. "Second, Bob Atwood would have to agree to be my press secretary. Third, Jesse Carr would have to agree to serve as my labor commissioner. Fourth, Tom Fink would have to contribute two million dollars to my campaign. Fifth, polls would have to show I had 99 and 44/100ths percent of the popular vote. Sixth, legislators would have to grant me total dictatorial powers in passage of my proposals. And finally, seventh, my wife would have to promise not to leave me."

Two days later, there appeared a news story headlined: "Hammond to Consider Running Again?" The story cited my seven conditions. For the next few days I received phone calls and letters, two of which contained campaign contributions, offering support from some folks who had not gotten beyond the headline.

A few days later, while having lunch at Hickel's Captain Cook Hotel, publisher Bob Atwood's second in command, Bill Tobin, came up and told me: "Bob says he's ready to go. Have you talked to Wally?"

Two days later, I'm told, an open letter appeared in Atwood's *Anchorage Times,* which in essence read: Dear Jay: I'm in if Fink comes up with the two million. Regards, Wally.

I greatly appreciated the good humor with which Atwood and Hickel responded to my facetious set of conditions. Bella was less amused: "Now all those deluded people who really *do* want you to run are going to blame *me* for keeping you from it."

"Both of them?" I asked.

PERHAPS MY GREATEST inducement for not running again lay in the remarkably kind and generous treatment I was accorded when no longer viewed as a political threat. A reporter, well aware of my thin margins of victory, once asked: "To what do you attribute your latter-day popularity?"

"Very simple," I told the reporter. "Everyone knows you can't believe a word a politician tells you. So I tell them what a *lousy* job I did as governor and mention my failures. This seems to trigger not only disbelief but prompts many to come to my administration's defense. Whereas, were I to make excuses or put a more positive spin on my efforts I'm sure I'd once again be assaulted."

Curious, but seemingly true. Even many who say they voted against me contend they are now great supporters. Of course, I've no delusions. After all, it's pretty hard to hate Santa Claus. Receipt of annual Permanent Fund dividend checks no doubt has done much to dull memories and to delude Alaskans into thinking I'm fully responsible.

While most politicians, even those once vigorously opposed to dividends, now clamor to at least climb aboard Santa's sleigh and insist they helped provide the reindeer power required to deliver those checks, some resent I also get most credit for creation of the fund itself. Old-time lobbyist Alex Miller, present at the fund's birth and perhaps more familiar than anyone with what went on behind the scenes in Juneau, once groused: "You take entirely too much credit for creation of the Permanent Fund."

"No, no," I countered, "I'm *given* entirely too much credit for creation of the Permanent Fund. It would have never happened without the efforts of a number of others."

"Well, then, who really is the father of the Permanent Fund? You? Earl Hillstrand? Oral Freeman? Hugh Malone?

"You are, Alex. Along with thousands of other Alaskans who voted to enshrine it in our constitution."

The Alaskans who collectively seem most friendly or forgiving to me are African Americans. Seldom do I pass an African American who does not recognize me and offer kindly comment. This is surprising, since at one time my staff and campaign supporters feared I had alienated the black community beyond redemption.

The first occasion came while I was still in the Legislature. I had opposed a resolution requesting Congress to declare Martin Luther King's birthday a national holiday. I felt such a holiday would not only incur undue expense but also add to racial divisiveness, since at that time Dr. King was a controversial figure, not esteemed by most Americans as he is today. My vote against the King resolution was painful because I knew it would be interpreted as bigotry, since certainly all bigots would so vote.

In trying to explain this wasn't my motivation, I said I'd not even support creation of a national holiday in behalf of my father, whom I esteemed above all men. "National holidays," I said, "should be reserved for the extremely rare individual who is held in exceptionally high regard by virtually all." It was some years before this was the case for Dr. King and a holiday in his name was created. In the meanwhile, my comments did little to segregate me from those who might have been redneck bigots. All "no" voters were lumped together in a newspaper editorial captioned "Day of Infamy" and edged in funereal black.

My second indiscretion occurred during my first month as governor when I fired the only African American appointed by the previous adminis-tration. J. P. Jones was a member of the Alaska Human Rights Commis-sion—a fiercesome-looking critic with a mau-mau hairdo, who repeatedly charged that I had backed down from an alleged commitment to put African Americans in my cabinet. Each time I would patiently explain why he was mistaken. That is, until the last time.

It was during a heavily attended meeting at which the commission was to discuss the findings of a survey to determine the administration's success at increasing minority and female hiring. Aware the survey showed we had done well, I anticipated accolades from commission members. In-stead old J. P. launched into his usual assault.

"Yeah, you increased females in your cabinet by 100 percent," he said. "Big deal. Egan had one. You have two. And that 65 percent increase in minority hire is made up almost entirely of Natives. What's more, you promised to put blacks in your cabinet and you did not!"

Previously I had taken the time to remind J. P. that when I appeared before the NAACP and the Alaska Black Caucus, I clearly had not promised to put blacks in my cabinet. Rather, in response to whether I intended to do so, I had stated: "Not simply because they are black. However, I have to admit to this degree of prejudice: show me a black with the same qualifica-tions as a white and I'll appoint him. But I don't know many members of the black community, so I'll have to rely on you folks for recommendations. Please send any you might have."

The only recommendation I ever received came from an individual who recommended himself for a cabinet post. Inquiry into his credentials revealed an unsavory history of spousal abuse and a few other legal infrac-tions, for which he was currently in jail.

When J. P. Jones again erroneously charged I had broken my word, I'd had enough. "J.P., you're telling it like it isn't," I told him at the meeting. "I wouldn't tolerate that in a white man, so I'm going to give you equal treat-ment. You're canned!"

Several staff members later assumed my action had alienated black voters. But the only direct response I received from the black community was from an individual who felt J. P. too militant to advance concerns of his race and therefore endorsed my action. But that was not to be my last confrontation with the overzealous J. P.

As a gimmick in my 1978 reelection campaign, my Fairbanks office had advertised that the governor would scrub the first three cars arriving at a local car wash. Guess who was first in line. There sat J. P. behind a big grin, barely discernible through a bug-begrimed windshield in an ancient truck seemingly held together only by the crud encrusting it. I dutifully gave the old rattletrap a through washing on the exterior and would have shot the hose into the interior also had J. P. not frantically rolled up the window, requiring me to seek another portal.

This incident caused me to view J. P. in a far more favorable light thanks to his sense of humor, an attribute of which I had been unaware. Years later I was touched to receive an invitation to his daughter's wedding, and regretted having shoved that hose up his exhaust pipe, thereby requiring his truck to be towed away.

IF EVER I PONDERED a third go at the governor's chair, I had only to look back on my life to find sufficient reason to "just say no." My first campaign for governor had served as another example of an affliction that has always plagued me. I'd start out doing something new with remarkable success, perhaps unaware it was unusual to do so well at the start. Then, after praising me for my performance, people would look forward to seeing me get better and better. And I, despite diligence, practice, and determination, would proceed to get worse and worse, in a downward spiral. The harder I tried, the faster I'd slide. I call this unhappy attribute "disgrace under pressure." So it was that after sweeping through the primary election, I just squeaked through the general.

This condition first became evident when I was thirteen years old. My cousins Billy and Jimmy Azer had snitched one of their dad's golf clubs, and together we sneaked onto the local golf course. Some indulgent golfers taking a breather told us to go ahead and tee up ahead of them on a par five hole. This was the first time I'd ever set foot on a golf course, though I had whacked a ball about in a cow pasture a time or two using an old mashie, the sole club owned by my father.

Swinging the club like a baseball bat, I stepped into the ball and smacked it a country mile to the applause of my audience. A second shot put me within ten feet of the cup. The third dropped it in. An eagle!

Having never played before, I did not know the term, but it soon was apparent from comments made by witnesses that eagles were rare birds indeed. Accordingly, all eyes were on me as I teed off for the next hole. Twenty-seven strokes later I finally dropped the ball in the cup, sinking as well any speculation I was a budding Arnold Palmer. Though having golfed a few times since, I never again shot a *birdie*, much less an eagle.

So it was with shot-putting. The first time I tried to shot-put was in Navy preflight school at Chapel Hill, North Carolina. Having no idea of proper form,

I launched the sixteen-pound ball forty-six and a half feet. "Wow!" gasped the track coach. "Once I teach you proper form you'll do great." He had once held the indoor world's record, which at the time was something like fifty-two feet, and he made me aware I had done something unusual.

For the next several weeks my coach labored to hone my technique. At that time this involved simply hopping straight across the ring, rather than performing the explosive spins of today. I hurled that iron ball several hundred times in an effort to beat my first attempt. I never did.

The same thing happened with bowling. One afternoon I accompanied a group of cadets on a stroll around the Corpus Christi Naval Air Station. We passed a bowling alley that displayed a sign saying: "Free Carton of Cigarettes for Weekly High Score." All the cadets except me wanted to bowl.

"Gee, guys," I protested, "I've only bowled once before and that was at age fourteen."

Nevertheless I reluctantly agreed to join them. To my surprise, rolling strikes seemed remarkably easy. I hurled one strike after another. My final score: 232.

"Never bowled before?" chided the low scorer, who had to pick up the tab. "What a crock! You've obviously done this a time or two."

"Just once, I swear." I inadvertently went on to prove my point and live up to my normal "disgrace under pressure." In the very next game, with the same ball, on the same alley, I bowled a 97. Never again was I to bowl more than 200, even though after learning the rules of the game and polishing my technique I've bowled scores of times since.

The same curse dogged me when I tried out years later for the University of Alaska Fairbanks rifle team. The first time I shot for score with a small bore rifle, I broke the school record and was elected team captain. A year and several thousand rounds later I managed to equal, but never exceeded, my first score.

So it was with skeet shooting. During flight training at Love Field in Dallas, prospective fighter pilots were required to shoot five rounds of skeet in preparation for aerial gunnery practice. I had previously fired only six shells, years earlier when a friend had loaned me his single-shot 12-gauge. But at Love Field, busting clay pigeons seemed easy. In those five rounds of skeet I averaged twenty-one kills—never less than eighteen, and once twenty-five out of twenty-five.

At my next stage of training, at Corpus Christi, we were again required to shoot several rounds of skeet. This time, however, we had to wear shooting glasses. To my disgust, most of my birds flew off unscathed. I averaged about twelve per round. "Must be those glasses are fouling me up," I consoled myself. But later, even without these glasses and with plenty of practice, I never again broke more than eighteen birds in a round.

And so it goes. No doubt the same would occur if I attempted to run for office again.

The 28 golden years? My gluteus!

My golden girl Bella and I "maturing" in her pansy patch.

THERE ARE FEW THINGS more depressing than some old gaffer whining about his decrepitudes. I once swore I'd never inflict on others clinical dissertations on the state of my gastrointestinal tract or which creaking joint most commanded attention. Yet of late, I dwell overmuch on these sorry issues.

In my defense, I bring them up now only in the hope they may help pry open minds that may be unaware of procedures not revealed by most traditional medical doctors. Lamentably the gulf between traditionalists and alternative medical practitioners still yawns, though it steadily closes as more becomes known of nutrition and supplements. In exploring that chasm, I've had some remarkable experiences that compel me to recount them for consideration of those who may be unaware of the potentials and pitfalls found on each side of that chasm. My experiences are but anecdotal, comprising a mixed bag of inconclusive evidence, but they beg for additional investigation.

My odyssey began in the mid-1980s when I received a newsletter from a Dr. Julian Whitaker, touting the benefits of glucosamine sulfate and chondroitin for easing joint pain. Since my mail, like that of every senior citizen, overflows with flyers touting nostrums that will let you live to be 125, have sex thirty times a week, kick cancer, regain the heart and lungs of a teenager, and shrink the prostate from the size of a coconut to that of a kumquat, my inclination was to chuck it. However, aching joints overruled that decision. I placed an order. After taking glucosamine and chondroitin for two months, I realized significant relief. I've since told dozens of others of my experience. Most who tried the products reported similar results.

Placebo, or psychosomatic effect? Hardly in the case of my grandkid's rottweiler, which was suffering from hip dysplasia. Her condition had so degenerated she would often collapse in pain, and we contemplated having her put to sleep. As an alternative I suggested they ask their vet to try glucosamine. He did, and Greta rapidly improved. She ran around like a puppy for three more years. I learned that veterinarians had long used the substance, which only recently had been approved for human use.

When my friend Bill Sheldon told me he was feeling increasing joint pain while running, I suggested he try both glucosamine and chondroitin, which are believed to help rebuild cartilage in joints. I cautioned him to give them at least two months to work. He later told me what happened: "I took the products for two solid months and they did nothing for me. But then they kicked in. I couldn't believe the relief. Never again will I be without them."

Though scoffed at by many traditional doctors just a few years ago, glucosamine and chondroitin are prime ingredients in products now widely advertised for arthritis relief and are often recommended by physicians who once considered them nothing but snake oil.

It was from Whitaker's newsletters I first learned of saw palmetto and other natural herbs for alleviating prostate problems. These substances also have subsequently been widely accepted by many who once deemed them worthless. So impressed were we with Whitaker's recommendations that Bella and I spent a week at his Wellness Clinic in Newport Beach, California. While there we learned more of Whitaker's background and efforts to promote alternative medicine. The son of a renowned heart surgeon, Whitaker had been intent upon following in his father's footsteps. After receiving his medical degree and performing several heart surgeries, however, he became convinced there often were more effective, less dangerous, and less-expensive treatment alternatives ignored by medical practitioners locked into the cut-and-stitch mindset.

One treatment employed by Whitaker was chelation. *Chela* in Greek means "to claw." Many years ago, German scientists discovered they could infuse into the blood stream a substance, known as EDTA, that "clawed" out heavy metals, such as lead and mercury. An unanticipated side effect was that the treatment appeared to correct heart conditions attributable to clogged arteries, the prime excuse for angioplasty or heart surgery.

I've since met many people who have had heart surgery and were scheduled for more, but instead chose chelation treatment. All without exception felt chelation was not only far less traumatic but also was much more effective while being far less costly. After undergoing chelation myself, I found ample reason to plead for its full evaluation to determine if it might be used more widely as an alternative. But more on that later. First bear with me while I relate some other experiences that may have implications for you as you "mature."

IN THE SPRING OF 1995 I was reading in bed at our homestead when I experienced chest pains that grew increasingly severe. I was about to fly myself into Anchorage to see a doctor, but concluded that under the circumstances it would not be too smart for me to pilot a plane. Bella agreed and called our friend Glen Alsworth by radio, and Glen flew me to Anchorage, where I entered the Alaska Regional Hospital intensive care unit. I spent the next several days undergoing tests, which indicated I had no significant heart problems. However, one evening a nurse scurried in to announce: "There's been some changes. I'm going to call the doctor."

"Changes? What sort of changes?" She did not elaborate.

The doctor announced I had gone into atrial fibrillation, a very rapid and irregular heartbeat that fails to pump sufficient blood from the upper heart chamber to the lower. "Nothing too serious. People can live for years with it. However, we'll try to correct it with medication. If that doesn't work we'll cardiovert you."

Three days of medication failed to correct the condition, so I was scheduled for cardioversion the following morning. That evening I watched a late-night movie in which a patient went into ventricular fibrillation while undergoing back surgery. In attempting cardioversion, they hit him with the electrical defibrillating paddles four or five times. After bouncing off the walls and ceiling like a freshly caught flounder, he expired. As they pulled the sheet over his head I snapped off the TV and spent a restive night contemplating my own scheduled paddling.

It proved anticlimactic, so I thought. After a general anesthetic that put me out for a couple of minutes, one boot with the paddles shocked my heart back into synch. The next day I was discharged and flew home feeling almost as good as new. The following morning, however, I awoke with weakness in my left deltoid muscle, numbness in three fingers of my left hand, and a sensation like an intense sunburn radiating down my right side.

Worse yet, I found that although the call was urgent, I could not tap a kidney. As time elapsed, anxiety rose to alarm and then anguish. We again called Lake Clark Air, and pilot Joel Natwick flew me back to the hospital, where a urologist told me that my problem was caused by an enlarged prostate. (Biopsies proved it noncancerous.)

It was later concluded by neurologists that both my difficulty in voiding and the burning feeling down my right side were probably due to a small spinal cord stroke, apparently caused by failure to have been given a blood thinner at least a couple of days before my cardioversion. Though now obligatory, I'm told that back then it was optional. Intense burning and numbness on my right leg remains unabated—a constant reminder of this episode. Sure saves on the long underwear, though. I can tolerate them only on my left leg, so by cutting each pair of long underwear in half, I double their life span.

A medication called Hyprin provided prostate relief, but at the dosage required to be effective, I found myself "flying" about three feet off the ground. And as far as actual flying while piloting an airplane, the urologist said: "You can still fly, but you'll have to have someone with you."

Since use of aircraft is crucial to living on our remote roadless homestead, I asked my urologist if there were other treatments as an alternative to the drugs.

"Well, there's the traditional 'roto-rooting,' where we bore out the piping," he explained. "Or perhaps you'd like to consider a microwave procedure used in Europe for some time but only recently approved in this country. Trouble is we don't have the equipment to do it up here yet and there's only a couple of places back East where you can get it done. However, there's a clinic in Windsor, Ontario, that might be most convenient."

"Sounds good to me. I'm heading to Windsor."

A weekend trip to the Windsor Prostate Clinic involved but an hour in the doctor's office where I was subjected to microwaving. (To those with inquiring minds: No, you don't crawl into the microwave; it crawls into you.) The treatment, known as transurethral microwave thermotherapy, proved almost totally benign and very effective. No adverse side effects were experienced. I'm told the equipment is now available at most major hospitals, and treatment time has been reduced to but one half-hour. To my surprise I find that few men with enlarged- prostate problems have heard of this procedure and instead subject themselves to the painful hazards and sometimes debilitating side effects accompanying surgical treatment. If you're wearing a groove between bedroom and bath in repeated nocturnal treks to the head, microwaving may be worth checking out. One caution, however: I read an article claiming that improper use of the microwave procedure can parboil the prostate, so make sure a "master chef" is at the controls.

During this period I had to listen to any number of stories about other guys with the same condition. Like the story of the old fellow who asked his urologist for help:

"Well," the doctor said, "I can prescribe medication. Try it for six weeks and then come back."

The fellow was back in six weeks to report.

"Thanks, Doc, that stuff really works. Now instead of getting up five or six times a night, I only get up once or twice. But I have to tell you, when I do, an amazing thing happens. When I get ready to go, God turns on the light for me. And when I'm finished God turns it off."

"Oh, oh," thought the doctor. "The old boy seems to be hallucinating. I'd best tell his wife."

He called her to explain the problem. "Your husband says he now only gets up a couple of times a night but when he does, God turns the light on for him and when he's finished God turns it off."

"Oh no," she said. "Now he's peeing in the refrigerator!"

29 Root of my problems

No longer physically able to do anything worthwhile like cutting wood, I reluctantly left our Lake Clark homestead temporarily to seek medical help, both traditional and supplemental. Heidi Hammond photo

MONTANA'S CRUSTY OLD COWBOY artist Charlie Russell once groused: "Old Father Time brings you lots of gifts you'd just as soon pass up and takes away many you'd like to hang on to." During the winter of 1999 I came to learn just what he meant.

My shoulders and knees started aching so badly I needed help dressing. I could hardly climb into a car, much less an aircraft. Barely able to walk a hundred feet at a time, a cane became my close companion. Unable to bend sufficiently to put socks on, I used a device to pull them up by attached ropes. For almost six months I failed to get a decent night's sleep, and many nights I slept not at all. Pain pills and sleeping potions were ineffective. Since my condition continued to deteriorate, I had to leave our Lake Clark homestead. I'd gone from cane to crutch and appeared bound for a wheelchair.

One Saturday morning, Bella and I tuned in for the first time to a radio call-in show conducted by Dr. Robert Jay Rowan of Anchorage. I'd not met the doctor, but I recalled the firestorm of abuse heaped on Governor Hickel when he appointed Rowan to the state medical board. Rowan is an outspoken advocate of alternative medical treatment, and though he is a licensed MD, he was branded a quack by some of his traditionalist colleagues. He came across on the radio as articulate, well-informed, and intelligent. What really grabbed my attention, however, was his story about a woman who had been suffering from debilitating back pain. Her doctor recommended surgery. Wishing a second opinion, she saw Dr. Rowan.

"The first thing I asked," Rowan said, "was 'have you ever had a root canal?'"

She said she had.

"I located two," Rowan continued, "and injected them with procaine; whereupon she virtually leaped off the examining table, exclaiming: 'What in the world have you done? The pain is all gone!'"

Rowan explained that many times people with painful joints have had root canals that went awry, causing infection that erodes the jawbone, creating what is termed a cavitation. From these, toxic materials go into one's system, bringing on all sorts of problems. Once cleaned out, he asserted, the patient often experiences great relief.

"Gee, I wonder if that could possibly be my problem?" I asked Bella.

"Go in and find out," she said.

TWO WEEKS LATER, after another sleepless night, I staggered into Rowan's office to meet him for the first time. A slim, fit dynamo of a man, he was given to flitting from patient to patient while discoursing on all manner of subjects. Rowan's eyes displayed a disquieting Svengalian intensity that grew as he launched into a scathing critique of his traditionalist colleagues who refused to acknowledge any merit in alternative (Rowan termed them supplemental) treatments until compelled to do so by overwhelming evidence far beyond that required of drugs or surgical procedures.

"For years they scoffed at vitamin and mineral supplements, contending all you had to do was eat a balanced diet. But of course nobody does, and now many supplements are prescribed by the mainstream. All many traditional doctors do is treat the symptoms and not the disease. For example, they'll prescribe heart bypass surgery and tell you you're a ticking time bomb unless you immediately go under the knife, rather then first try alternative treatments to eliminate problems for which they prescribe surgery or angioplasty. Why? Because they fear their multibillion-dollar heart surgery rice bowl might be broken if folk learned of these alternatives."

His dissertation was remarkably similar to that of Dr. Whitaker, and the passion with which Rowan sermonized made clear why traditionalists did not warmly embrace him.

When I explained my condition, Rowan asked if *I* had ever had any root canals. I told him I had but could not recall their location. To find them, Rowan undertook a diagnostic procedure that made me think of tarot reading or Ouiji board consultation. He had me extend my right arm and then, with my left forefinger, touch each tooth in turn. As I touched each tooth, he attempted to lever down my right arm.

This method was one of the alternative diagnostic approaches that look at first like two parts mumbo jumbo and one part snake oil. How in the world could someone make an accurate finding simply by tugging down on my arm while I touched a tooth? However, I didn't scoff at this approach because some years earlier, I had witnessed a demonstration that at least hinted at such a possibility.

One evening during my tenure in Juneau, a group of about fifty people came to the governor's house to witness a demonstration organized by the state's Division of Corrections. It was designed to demonstrate the impact on prisoners of various color schemes. The invited lecturer first requested a gargantuan state trooper to come forward. After all six-foot-five and 250 pounds of him had lumbered to the front of the room, he was asked to stare at a sheet of blue paper for fifteen seconds.

"Now hold out your right arm and see if you can keep me from tugging it down," the lecturer told him. The behemoth had no trouble resisting the downward pressure.

The trooper was then asked to stare at a sheet of pink paper for fifteen seconds. This time when he held his arm out, the lecturer easily pulled it down with two fingers.

"Wait a minute," the astonished trooper said. "Try that again." Once more he could not keep his arm from being easily levered downward.

The lecturer didn't exactly explain how this bizarre effect worked, but he did point out its value in law enforcement and prisons.

The lecturer could not explain why this bizarre effect worked, but he did explain its value to law enforcement.

"We find choice of color used in correction facilities can have great significance. For example, when first apprehended, suspects are usually angry, frightened, and frustrated. If brought into a room painted pink, they become more placid and manageable than if brought into a room painted blue."

My subsequent reading of a scientific explanation of the effect of colors only confused me, but I was sufficiently convinced that should I ever take up professional wrestling I'd wear pink tights and insist my opponent wear blue.

This experience made me a little more trusting of the unusual method used by Dr. Rowan. As I touched tooth after tooth, I was able to easily resist his downward pressure on my arm. Suddenly, however, as I moved to an incisor, he pulled my arm down with ease. "Ah, there's one." I went from tooth to tooth until he found another. To my disappointment, however, at first injections of procaine did nothing to improve my condition.

"I still recommend you see a dental surgeon who performs cavitation procedures," Rowan said. "He may have some suggestions." I agreed and made an appointment with Dr. Leland Cho in Anchorage. (X-rays later taken by Dr. Cho showed that Rowan had correctly identified my root canals.)

AFTER ANOTHER SLEEPLESS NIGHT, I drove in pain to Dr. Cho's office. En route I had to stop in order to stand for relief of the burning on my right side, which had been aggravated by whatever new problems I had. Hardly able to stagger into his office, I almost left immediately when I was met by an African American male dressed in surgical whites who resembled Mike Tyson. "Oh, oh," I thought, "is this the dentist, or simply the muscle that holds you in the chair?" It turned out he was a dental assistant with an exceptionally personable manner and abundant knowledge gleaned from years of experience.

After helping me into the dental chair and bibbing me up, we awaited Dr. Cho. When he arrived, I was again inclined to depart in haste. The doctor was Chinese and looked barely out of his teens. Upon learning he was well into his thirties and indeed a qualified oral surgeon, I relaxed—until he explained the procedure.

"We'll determine which areas appear to need treatment, then drill into the jawbone and extract all the diseased bone tissue. We'll fill the cavitations with a mixture of bovine bone and a synthetic material and stitch you up. There are five suspect areas indicated by the x-rays."

The procedure proved less traumatic than its description. Several shots of procaine were administered, one tooth that had been given a root canal was extracted, and another cavitation was excavated and filled. While driving home I experienced little of the burning sensation on my right side. More remarkable, for the first time in almost six months I had a splendid night's sleep. The stiffness and pain in my shoulders and the back of my knees were gone.

In the morning I was able to put on my socks without the roped device I'd needed for months. I could walk almost normally without using my cane. I literally ran into Dr. Rowan's office that morning.

"Wow!" he said when he saw me. "I've never seen quite so dramatic an improvement."

"Doc, I know you've stirred up controversy in the past," I told him, "but as far as I'm concerned you're a candidate for canonization!"

Two days later, however, the pain and stiffness in shoulders and knees had returned and I was again staggering about with my cane. Subsequent treatments by Dr. Cho yielded the same results, except by then injections of procaine alone provided instant relief. So remarkable were the results that both Cho and Rowan videotaped the process. Within a minute or two of injection, I could feel the pain virtually flood out of my shoulders and knees and the stiffness would vanish. Previously unable to bend down, I could easily touch my toes and literally run. It was astounding, but unfortunately very short-lived. These amazing results occurred perhaps six times, but then the procaine ceased having any effect. I needed to try something else.

Meanwhile, material extracted from the cavitation beneath my No. 10 tooth was sent to a lab at the University of Kentucky, which analyzed it for toxins by implanting it beneath the skin of a rabbit. The rabbit died in three days. In checking a chart that showed parts of the anatomy affected by diseased material, I was astounded to note that at the top of the list of body parts affected by the No. 10 tooth were the shoulders and the back of the knees.

Dr. Rowan referred me to Dr. Douglas Cooke, a Wisconsin oral surgeon said to be most knowledgeable in such matters. Dr. Cooke said the benefits of cavitation procedures were sometimes short-lived when a person has incompatible metals in the mouth, such as mercury fillings. So I had Cooke remove four fillings and replace all bridges and crowns with compatible materials.

At the time of this dental surgery, I was feeling pain in my right arm and shoulder so intense I could sit for only a few moments before I had to move about to seek relief. As I sat in his chair, Dr. Cooke brought out a triggered device about the size of a cell phone; extending from this was a probe at the end of a wire. As he moved the probe to various parts of my right ear, he would ask me to pull the trigger, which focused a mild electrical charge on the target area. With but two or three tries he hit pay dirt. The pain completely vanished.

He repeated the process as needed about every five minutes. Each time the pain vanished but gradually returned. After five or six applications, the process no longer worked. Dr. Cooke likened the effect of the device to the pain-relieving benefits of acupuncture, another alternative treatment that many traditional medical doctors now recognize as helpful even if they cannot fully explain it.

ONE MONTH after the dental work by Dr. Cooke, I felt somewhat better but was still in considerable pain and sleeping fitfully. Several friends, including two traditional doctors, advised I go to Mayo Clinic, in Rochester, Minnesota.

I did and was probed from stem to stern. No orifice was left uninvaded. I was subjected to every conceivable (and many inconceivable) tests. One test compelled me to break a promise I'd made to Dr. Rowan. The doctor is opposed to such things as fluoridation, various inoculations, and even mammograms, and he is sorely criticized by the traditional medical fraternity for these views. One day he read to a group of patients, including me, an article that seemed to support his contention that mammograms can be hazardous. "Well, Governor," he said to me, "what do you think of that?"

"You sure convinced me," I replied. "I ain't going to have one."

Well, guess what? Back at Mayo, I had some irritation in my left nipple and was directed to have a mammogram. Upon entering a waiting room, the dozen or so females present stared suspiciously at me, the lone male. When it came my turn, I was virtually suspended by a left pectoral muscle hard-pressed to fill an "A" cup. The tissue was biopsied and mercifully proved negative for cancer for which I was immensely grateful, though somewhat disappointed that the diagnosis also served to cancel my invitation to attend self-examination classes, to which I'd somewhat looked forward.

Rather than revealing the cause of my problems, all the tests at the Mayo Clinic simply eliminated one possible cause after another. The prime benefit was to learn what I did *not* have. For residual pain in my knees and shoulders, Mayo doctors prescribed a declining dose of cortisone. Fearing the drug's side effects, I began the regimen with reluctance. However, its effect was astounding. In the wake of Dr. Cooke's treatments I'd already begun to sleep at least an hour or two each night, but immediately after beginning the cortisone treatment I was able to sleep fairly comfortably four or five hours a night. I no longer dreaded going to bed.

After five months away, I was able to rejoin Bella at our Lake Clark home. However, this interlude was short-lived. Increasing pain in my right hip soon demoted me again from cane to crutch. On the recommendation of several friends I sought the services in Anchorage of Dr. Adrian Ryan, who basically advised that I needed a major overhaul. Simply kicking my tires and changing my oil would not be enough. I was scheduled for hip surgery.

During surgery my heart rate dropped to twenty beats per minute, prompting the implant of a pacemaker device to regulate my heartbeat. "Living as you do in a remote area," my cardiologist said, "I think it wise. Had that occurred at the lake you'd have probably had a major heart attack."

With ankle, back, knee, and hip overhauls, plus an electronic ticker, I am rapidly becoming bionic. Now all I need is a brain transplant and I should be good for another few thousand miles despite the sprung chassis and body rust.

This presumption, however, was dampened when on my seventy-eighth birthday, while stomping down the street, I met an old Eskimo friend I'd not seen in years.

"Just how old are you now?" he inquired.

Waving my cane, I chuckled: "Above the waist I'm thirty-five; below, I'm eighty-seven and a half."

He never even cracked a smile. "Oh, almost eighty-eight," he said.

At least I've remained consistent: In my teens, I could pass for much older. And by George, I *still* can.

30 Touring the twilight zone

Grandkids Jay, Lauren, and Nick help burnish the Golden Years.
Heidi Hammond photo

BETWEEN TRADITIONAL AND SUPPLEMENTAL medical practitioners, there remains a vast, if narrowing, gulf. I've spent much time exploring that netherworld and have made some startling discoveries. I have a doctor friend who labels alternative treatments 90 percent quackery—but he is thereby admitting that 10 percent may have merit. The most startling aspect of my own limited investigation of chelation, for example, is that without exception each of the more than two dozen prospective heart-bypass patients I've talked to who underwent chelation believe it helped them immensely. Some had endured as many as three heart surgeries and were scheduled for more when they decided they'd had enough and sought alternative treatment. Most claimed their regular doctors were astounded to find they no longer "required" surgery or angioplasty.

Among chelation's most enthusiastic advocates is former governor Wally Hickel, who certainly must be doing something right. In his eighties and seemingly more vigorous than ever, he asserts he's simply into his third forty-year life span.

In my own case, prior to undergoing chelation I was in atrial fibrillation, with a faulty heartbeat, and took medication for high blood pressure. Upon completing the chelation regimen I was no longer fibrillating; my heartbeat was regular and my blood pressure normal.

Among the patients I met while undergoing chelation was Sam. His doctors had told him there was nothing more they could do for him and gave him no more than another six months to live. In the process of learning this prognosis, Sam had exhausted his bank account. Sam told me he had always wanted to visit Alaska, and suddenly saw a way to visit the state and perhaps replenish his estate. The way Sam tells it, he told his son that he was about to die and asked him to go to Alaska with him to help him with his plan.

"I want to find the biggest grizzly bear in Alaska and then attempt to kick his butt," Sam told his son. "What's more, I want you to video the action. I'm going to die anyway so I've nothing to lose; but whether I survive the encounter or not, you'll have something you can sell for lots of money."

I assume his son was less than enthusiastic about this proposition, but nonetheless he did accompany Sam to Alaska. By then disease had so taken its toll that Sam could barely walk, much less try to track down a grizzly. While here he encountered someone who suggested he visit Dr. Rowan.

"He saved my life," Sam said. "It's as simple as that." After but two chelation treatments, Sam felt wonderful. Hence he happily abandoned his search for that monster grizzly and returned home to Portland, where his doctor expressed amazement at his improvement and said, "I don't know what you're doing but keep doing it." That was several years ago.

Another old fellow who was listening to Sam told of a similar experience. He claimed that a few years before, he too had been given only a few months to live but improved wondrously after chelation and no longer needed his second prescribed triple bypass operation.

One problem with the use of chelation seems to be that not all treatments are uniform. For example, when I asked Sam why he did not seek treatment in his home state of Oregon, he said he had, but that it almost killed him. "I don't know what the difference was," he told me, "but I didn't want to take any more chances." Such occurrences naturally have led traditional physicians to view chelation with skepticism.

Although Medicare and other health insurance will cover the great expense of heart surgery, insurers will not pay one cent for chelation. Something seems terribly wrong here. Either chelation works or it doesn't. Of the dozens of people I know who have successfully undergone it, many had previously undergone heart surgery. One old fisherman friend, Chuck Allan, from Naknek, had an incredible ten operations, but after chelation did not need the scheduled eleventh. Nearly all chelation patients I spoke with had been told they needed additional surgery. Most said they would never have had their first surgery had they known of chelation and other alternative treatments. None regretted having undergone alternative treatments. What goes on here?

Make of it what you will. What I make of it is that chelation should be thoroughly evaluated. The treatment is scoffed at by many traditional medical practitioners as, at best, an unproven waste of money and, at worst, potentially dangerous quackery. But this alternative approach to treating heart disease has convinced me and many others of its benefits. I find it distressing that this promising alternative has not been subjected to intensive, unbiased evaluation and then widely publicized as either effective or not. If chelation proves as effective as anecdotal evidence indicates, it seems almost criminal to not acquaint the public with its potential.

Some traditionalists contend I experienced nothing but a placebo effect from both the dental cavitation procedure and chelation. However, for me to believe that to be the case requires greater gullibility than does believing the benefits were directly attributable to the procedures. Over the years, if I've learned anything it is to keep an open mind on subjects that at first may seem outlandish. For example, innumerable experiences with telepathy, many of which I recounted in my autobiography *Tales of Alaska's Bush Rat Governor,* perhaps did most to dislodge skepticism. They compelled me to recognize that simply because I failed to understand something, I should not clamp my mind shut against the possibility it might have validity. Curiously, as I've grown older and less skeptical, telepathic experiences have become far less frequent, if not less persuasive. I'll recount but the most recent.

During December 1999, Bella and I accepted the invitation of friends Kent and Jenny Dawson to spend time at their Palms Springs retreat, where many roadways are named after notables from the entertainment world. When we saw Fred Waring Way, I remarked to Bella that Fred Waring had been a bandleader who conducted a group called The Pennsylvanians when I attended Penn State back in the forties. I then mentioned a fellow student, Jimmy Layden, who had gone through basic flight training with me. Jimmy, a fine musician himself, took great pride in having worked with Waring upon occasion.

Though I'd not thought of Jimmy Layden for over fifty years, to my astonishment the very next day he called me from his home back East.

"What in the world prompted you to call and how did you locate me"? I asked.

"Well," he said "yesterday for some reason I suddenly started thinking of you and thought I'd try to find your number on the Internet. I called the number I came up with and got your daughter, Heidi. She gave me this one."

Coincidence? I don't think so.

MOST FOLKS I ENCOUNTERED undergoing alternative medical treatment were in their sunset years and doing their best to fend off sundown. Some did so with astounding courage, others with depressing melancholy. When one exceeds the biblically allotted three score years and ten, it's natural to reflect increasingly on mortality. Years flash by with increasing tempo and we suddenly realize we perhaps have only a couple of years left, possibly five, but not likely ten. Where did all those other years go?

In youth I used to wonder what old age would be like. Does one actually *feel* old mentally? Or does one retain a self-image several years younger than the chronological age? I suspect most, like myself, have a mental self-image of someone inside who is thirty years younger and would like to come out and caper. One starts reading obituaries and attending funerals of folks, most of whom are shockingly younger than yourself. This can lead to morbid preoccupation with one's prospective departure.

It's odd that most people should so fear death. After all, believers of most religious faiths have assurance the soul survives and will experience a glorious hereafter. On the other hand, those not so persuaded presumably believe they have little to fear but the blessed oblivion of deep dreamless sleep since they acknowledge neither heaven nor hell. So what's the big deal?

Its not the *assurance* of death so much as the *manner* that niggles the mind at three in the morning when the specter of one's mortality scrolls like a dark shroud up from the foot of the bed to smother a pleasant dream. What does the grim reaper intend to pull off the shelf in his little shop of horrors to dump in your lap? Will a fat tumor, a stroke, a seizure, or something more exotic from his limitless stock send you spinning off into the void?

Our friend Elisabeth Kubler-Ross, a woman of exceptional dedication and wisdom, was convinced by studies of death and dying that an afterlife continues when our time on Earth is through. Several books on research conducted by others, most of whom assert they at first were totally skeptical, seem to confirm her conclusions. These books report on people who have come back from near-death, out-of-body experiences to clearly describe their departure from this world. Most of these people tell of entering a tunnel and seeing at the end of it a brilliantly lighted, benevolent being radiating love and eradicating fear. Another common denominator is that most of them assert they will never again fear dying.

Were these experiences truly the result of exposure to an afterlife, simply a short-circuiting of the synapses, or perhaps some glandular secretion pumped into the system to mercifully sedate one into acceptance of the inevitable? Fascinating questions for which one cannot know the answers until the final test.

In my case, should I depart tomorrow, I'd not feel shortchanged. I've had a life I would swap for no other with a wife, family, and friends I cherish more with each passing year. What more can one ask? However, I confess there are times when I'd drag my feet over that cosmic threshold. These may occur in the spring when grayling return to Miller Creek; or a wedge of snow geese slice high through Lake Clark Pass to westward natal nesting grounds; or the sun, about to sizzle out in the North Pacific, flames the snow peaks to the east; or when at sundown a lone wolf ghosts through the willows not far from our cabin, arousing the dogs from their slumbers to answer the mournful howl from one of their kind choosing not to come into the campfire's glow.

Those dragging feet get most heavy, however, when one of the grandkids hugs my creaking carcass and tells me they love their old Uppa. At those moments eighty years of accumulated stress and strain slough off and for a fleet instant I sense a faint glint of immortality. Ah, then? Then, despite my unfair share of abundant blessings, and years, this ancient Irish lament may squirm forth to haunt me: "Lord, ye were perhaps a wee bit unkind to have made thy hills and thy dales so beautiful, and the days of thy shepherd so few."

Index

A

Abortion, as a political issue, 103
Alaska, constitution, 67—68; finances, 83,
    105—108, 137, 139—141; fish and game board,
    68; gambling, 77—78; governor, 67—68, 108,
    111—113, 116—119, 122—128, 133, 144;
    legislature, 65—68, 70—75, 77—79, 83—86,
    88—91, 94—98, 101—103, 105—109, 152—153;
    myths, 137; permanent fund, 112—113, 119,
    138—141, 167, 170
Alaska National Interest Land Conservation Act,
    143—144, 148—149
Alsworth, Babe, 37—39
Alsworth, Mary, 37—38
Arctic National Wildlife Refuge, and oil, 143—144,
    145—146, 147
Arm wrestling, 117
Atomic detonation, Amchitka, 101—102
Atwood, Robert, 46, 90—91

B

Barnes, Ramona, 163
Bass, Howie, 33—34
Bears, 27—31, 33—35
Begich, Nick, 103
Beginner's luck, 172—173
Belcher, Dixie, 126—127
Binkley, Jim, 71—72
Blodgett, Bob, 70—72
Boyko, Edgar Paul, 60—62, 118
Bristol Bay, protection of, 144, 146
Butrovich, John, 95—96

C

Campaigning, 94, 111—112, 116—118, 163—167
Carter, Jimmy, 143, 147—149
Cho, Leland, Dr., 182—183
Clarke, Bob, 122
Cooke, Douglas, Dr., 183—184
Cowper, Steve, 165

D

Dankworth, Ed, 113—114
Dawson, V. Kent, 123—124
Dicky, Don, 88—89
Dicostanza, Chuck, 55—57

E

Egan, William A. 67—68, 83—
    84, 108, 111—112

F

Fanning, Kay, 91
Fleck, Freddie, 25
Flying, 53—57, 58

G

Gallagher, Sterling, 124—125
Golly, Bill, 33
Grimek, John, 23—24

H

Hansen, Harold, 66
Harris, Jess, 72—73
Heetderks, Dee, Dr., 49
Hellenthal, John S., 70—71
Hickel, Wally, 84, 117—118,
    161, 167
Hoshimo, Michio, 34—35
Hunting, 30—31, 48—50, 151—
    152

I

Irwin, Bill, 71

J

Jensen, Charlotte, 29
Jensen, Dick, 29—30
Jensen, Gordon, 125—126
Jones, Bob ("Sea Otter"), 33
Jones, J.P., 171—172

K

Kay, Wendell, 72
King, Martin Luther, Jr., 170—171
Kleeshulte, Chuck, 123
Knowles, Tony, 143
Kreta, Father Peter, 57—58
Kubler-Ross, Elisabeth, 190

L

Lewis, Meriwether, 45—46
Lobbyists, 88—89

M

McConnaughey, Lucy, 30—31
McGill, Joe, 94
Medical treatments, 175—178, 180—185,
    187—189
Miller, Keith, 84, 108

N

National Audubon Society, 144
Nichols, Robert, 15—17
Nicholson, Larry, 48—49
Nusinginya, John, 79

O

Oil, pipeline route, 108—109; sale of
    Prudhoe Bay leases, 106—108;
        severance tax, 105; tanker traffic, 106,
    108, 109
Outhouses, 157—158

P

Phillips, Vance, 103
Pignalberi, Marco, 163
Poland, Bill, 41
Public speaking, 158—161

R

Rader, John 70
Ray, Bill, 98

Reckley, Eve, 90
Reinwald, Jerry, 124
Rowan, Robert Jay, Dr., 180—182,
    183
Russia, tour, 126
Ryan, Adrian, Dr., 184

S

Shainlin, Herb, 91—92
Sheldon, Todd, 50—51
Snedden, Bill, 83
Sturgelewski, Arliss, 164—165
Sweeney, Dora, 78—79

T

Taylor, Warren, 65
Telepathy, 188—189
Tillion, Clem, 73—75, 101
Turner, Lana, 19—20

U

Udall, Mo, 143, 145

V

Vandergrift, Mike, 39—40
Vaughn, Norman, 43—44

W

Wassermen, Gloria, 25
Weight lifting, 22—25
Wettstone, Gene, 23—24
Whitaker, Julian, Dr., 175—176
Wiley, Warren, 127—128
Wolves, and predator control,
    131—134

Y

Young, Don, 119, 146—147

Z

Ziegler, John, Dr., 22—23